Penguin Education

Penguin Education Specials
General Editor: Willem van der Eyk

The school that I'd like
Edited by Edward Blishen

Penguin Education
Special

The school that I'd like

Edited by Edward Blishen

Published in collaboration with *The Observer*
Penguin Books

Penguin Books Ltd, Harmondsworth,
Middlesex, England
Penguin Books Inc., 7110 Ambassador Road,
Baltimore, Md 21207, U.S.A.
Penguin Books Australia Ltd, Ringwood,
Victoria, Australia

First published 1969
Reprinted 1970, 1971
Introductions copyright © Edward Blishen, 1969
Selection copyright © Penguin Books and contributors, 1969

Made and printed in Great Britain by
Hazell Watson & Viney Ltd,
Aylesbury, Bucks
Set in Linotype Juliana

Contents

Schools usually have one thing in common – they are
institutions of today run on the principles of yesterday.
15-year-old girl

At present, the main difference between secondary and primary
schools is that primary education is enjoyable and secondary
education is absolutely dreary and boring. Primary education . . .
that golden land where the revolution has at least partially taken
place. May it soon take place in our secondary schools !
13-year-old boy

School was not invented just for the little people to become the
same as the big people . . .
13-year-old girl

I am tired of hearing that the hope of my country lies in my
generation. If you give me the same indoctrination as a child,
how can you expect me to be any different from you?
15-year-old girl

Introduction

In December 1967, *The Observer* invited secondary schoolchildren to enter for a competition. They were to describe 'The School that I'd Like'. The response amounted to some half a million words, innumerable charts, collages, architectural or pseudo-architectural drawings. In another sense, it amounted to an enormous, remarkably good-humoured, earnest, frequently passionate and, at best, highly intelligent plea for a new order in our schools. No one who read through all those words could have believed for one moment that here were children seizing an opportunity to cock a snook at the *status quo*, for the sake of the snook. Juvenile irresponsibility was awfully hard to find. The radical note that was so pervasive was astonishingly steady, reasonable, and supported by instances. I have never read so much that was so full of complaints and criticisms, of schemes for imaginative innovation, and yet that was, as a whole, so very sober.

Certainly there was dross. More often than not this took the form of mass entries from schools where, clearly enough, the competition had been set as a class exercise. Here, one of the commonest criticisms made by all these young people was exemplified. 'I am too used to being told what to do,' wrote a fifteen-year-old boy. You could, in so many of these dutiful mass entries, detect the teacher who had told his pupils what to do. He had sketched out the ideal essay, and most of the entries followed it. They were stilted, unreal, and moved awkwardly from one given idea to the next. The only pleasure of reading them was to note the moment when some child, reaching out for the next official handhold, missed it and went hurtling downwards into honesty. But it must be said that entries of this kind formed only a small part of the total, and that there were many clearly inspired by an interested teacher on which he had set no stamp. Indeed, one of the discoveries made by those who read all these essays was that a few schools seem able to set their children free, intellectually, while others, having children of the same calibre and capacity, shut them up in the prison of a most dreadful conformity, so that you want to turn some sort of key and release them into the world of honest childhood.

I say 'some sort of key', as if the actual nature of the key were not fully described by these children themselves. They know themselves to be imprisoned, and they know the means of escape. First and foremost, they wish to learn. Well, obviously. But it is not the obvious, common connotation of the word 'learn' that they are concerned with. As things are, they say with shattering unanimity, learning is 'being told what to do' – and how to do it. The picture they build up of learning as it now most often is in the schools is one in which they, the pupils, are passive, sometimes very reluctant, recipients; the teachers are the providers – aided, if that is the word, by textbooks that also, oppressively if not dully, *provide*. It is this pattern of passively receiving, magisterially providing, that the children worry away at. Some do so at the naïvest level. School is boring; it is always a matter of listening to the teacher, never saying or doing anything of your own. Others put it more sophisticatedly. They too say that school is boring – it is the word that unites all the essays that allow themselves to be freely critical – but are subtler in their analysis of the cause. 'Everything learnt is second-hand if it comes from the teachers, and very often out-of-date and misleading if it comes from the books.' 'Children do not want to be taught at, but want to find out things for themselves.' 'The people who write textbooks do not make mistakes – and the best way to learn is by your own mistakes.' 'Instead of stuffing children into a classroom, within four boundaries, let them get out and see, feel, smell, hear and taste the subject.' 'Far better to replace constipated ways of teaching with more active lessons, with teachers and pupils discussing. ...'

Important to note that it is not just a few highly articulate and impatiently intelligent children who put such criticism at the centre of their dissatisfaction with schools as they are. From all the quarters of the educational scene it comes, this expression of children's longing to take upon themselves some of the burden of deciding what should be learnt, how it should be learnt: this desire to get closer to the raw matter of learning, not to be presented with predigested knowledge by teacher or textbook; above all, to learn by talking, debating, with the teacher as a senior confederate rather than the sole provider. They want excitement; they want a form of learning for which the word, for so many of them, is 'research'; they want to discover how to be responsible for themselves and their own ideas. They want simply to discover.

For many of them, there was a time when learning was discovery, and teachers seemed to be older partners, and that was in the primary school. There are children's words quoted in this book that glow with the memory of good primary school teaching, when you were fully involved – head, heart, imagination. It is a miserable thing that the step taken by so many of our children, when they pass to the secondary school, should be a step from excitement and acceptance into boredom and rejection.

But many of these children are kind about teachers. They argue that they ought to be better paid. They would not want them replaced by machines. They think they should be relieved of duties irrelevant to teaching itself. At the very least, they say, a teacher can introduce an element of surprise into any routine; at the best, he can communicate his own excitement about a subject, an activity, a matter of opinion. Yet, in general, and as things are, teachers are found guilty of remoteness, absence of sympathy for the young, attachment to trivial rules, failure to admit their ignorance or uncertainty. Part of the unhappiness – or lack of positive happiness – that many children find in their schools is due to the apparent inability of so many teachers to form with their pupils the relationships these children are seeking. And schools, they say, ought to be happy places.

The other general things these children have to say, together with many particular things, will be found in their proper place in this book in the children's own words. But it is worth jotting down the main points here, almost at random, because they make a picture that is so disconcerting, so exciting, and one that constitutes such an enormous challenge to the present usual pattern of schooling. The picture, composed of dominant views and the more interesting minority opinions, looks like this :

Of those who expressed a preference for any of the existing types of school, an overwhelming majority chose a comprehensive school, and wanted it to be mixed. They were against all kinds of segregation. Among the minority, more girls than boys wished to attend single-sex schools. A few were romantic reactionaries,

...nging for schools of immense antiquity, usually ivy-covered. Some girls thought of their schools in, as it were, boudoir terms, spending many pages lovingly over colour schemes. There were children who were brusque about buildings, believing they were of the last importance. Most, however, were either out of patience with school buildings as they are, or were profusely able to think of improvements. Most were tired of squareness: where an actual shape was suggested, nine times out of ten it was a round one. Domes were yearned for. Classrooms were hated, desks detested. They wanted gay decoration, and many wanted the decoration to bear the stamp of their own individuality. They wanted common rooms, rooms in which they could relax, and in general they wanted schools fit for leisure as for labour.

Examinations came under fire from all quarters: in them was seen the root of much evil. Examinations fitted into, or perhaps largely caused, that pattern that made the teacher the remote provider, the pupil the dyspeptic receiver. It was because of examinations that you could rarely flow over the strict and arid channel of the syllabus. Again, excellent sense was shown: it was necessary to assess achievement, but there were surely ways of doing it that would not clap the syllabus in irons or act merely as a measure of a single furious feat of memorization. Discipline was seen as a special aspect of relationships with teachers: in most schools, a tissue of tetchy rules; almost, one would think, a deliberate scheme to put up the backs of adolescents. Many pointed out that the secondary school child was at the very age when foolish rules had an explosive effect. He was also at an age when his desire for systems of discipline based on trust was at its most passionate.

They disliked prefects who, on the evidence of these essays, can rarely hope to be accepted as policemen by their peers. They raised the great, familiar groan against school food. There was not a good word to be said for homework – not because they were *against* work, but because they were *for* that other work the young are necessarily engaged in, the varied and untimetabled work of their leisure. Many were against timetables themselves, as a set of tiny boxes with a subject in each box. There was a great hatred of bells, which cut you off so often at a moment of interest, or before interest could even develop. You ought to be able to devote a whole day, a whole week to a piece of work, if it was really important. And why shouldn't they concentrate on subjects for which they felt they had an aptitude? Why were there so many moments of choice which involved losing a subject you had come to love?

About teaching machines, few of the children were really knowledgeable. They tended to think of them in science fiction terms – sometimes most attractively, as with the child who felt each desk could be fitted with a gadget that enabled conversations to be carried on with children in other countries; but it would have to be monitored, to ensure they did not descend to trivialities ('How many sisters and brothers have you?')* On the whole, the children felt there was a far greater place for modern teaching aids than is yet found for them in most schools; but they must not be allowed to dominate the scene. A fierce minority rejected school uniform *altogether*: most wanted to retain it in some brighter version, and to make it more responsive to changes in fashion. Almost without exception, they wanted smaller classes. Many wanted younger teachers, and would retire them at thirty-five, before crippling old age set in. And all references to religious instruction and the religious aspect of assemblies, with no exception at all, call for a complete change. There is scorn for what is seen, not just as a form of indoctrination, but also as the failure to grasp an opportunity to look at a wide range of religions and philosophies, to debate moral issues and affairs of the spirit.

It is that sort of picture; and one can construct it because on so many points, large and small, there is a most striking co-incidence of opinion. Standing out above everything else is the children's desire to teach themselves, rather than to be the passive targets of teaching: a great restlessness about classrooms, time-tables, the immemorial and so often inert routine of schools. The children seem to sense what their elders are slow to sense, that you enter the world of the late twentieth century ill-armed if all you have done is to submit, to some degree or other, to a pre-determined, pinched, examination-harried course of instruction,

* A curious (perhaps not uncommon) anxiety showed through in another entry: 'On every desk there is a little screen in which if you look through you can see your coats and bags in the cloakroom so they cannot be taken.'

from which in its nature most of the excitement and surprise of learning are excluded. They long to be excited, to be amazed by learning, since amazement seems to them to be a proper response to life. They are tired of being treated as children, in that sense of the word that means they are creatures from whom adults must be aloof or creatures who can be handled only if they are first trapped in a net of rules, mostly prohibitory. They want to learn to govern themselves. They want to take risks – lord, how anxious they are to be at risk, intellectually and emotionally, and how shameful it is that so many of them should find their teachers, the whole system of education, lacking in every kind of courage! They want to break down the walls of the school, to admit the wider world.

When I was reading these essays, the image of the prison returned to me again and again. We imprison the courage and the curiosity of our children. If we know that we do so, is it because we are afraid of all that energy, combined as it is with inexperience? Are we afraid that children set free can only be wild? Yet the evidence of all this writing is that our children are immensely anxious to be reasonable, to take account of practical difficulties. Some of these entries were dullish or dulled, but there was very little in them that was foolish. I can't imagine any educationist anxious to learn from what the children say who would not emerge from this book with his head full of perfectly firm and very sensible ideas.

Dividing the material into sections was not easy: much that was said, even in the course of a single sentence, had reference to many topics at once. It seemed important, though, to pick out, and to concentrate quotations on, the main themes. As will be seen, I found myself with substantial sections on teachers, teaching, the curriculum, moderate-sized sections on examinations, discipline and buildings, and a few interleaving sections that appear much slighter. I hope no one will undervalue these latter because of their brevity. It happens that the most characteristic points made about religious instruction in the schools could be represented within a few pages, but this fact does not mean that the children have only a slight interest in the teaching of religion. Far from it.

When I had marshalled my quotations into what seemed appropriate sections, I was left with a number that seemed to belong nowhere in particular, but that were, for one reason or another, too interesting to discard. Some were funny – deliberately or in a nicely unconscious way; a few made moving statements about experience at school; a few embodied agreeable but unpracticable fantasies; some were simply sensible by-the-ways. I make no apology for heaping these together into a final section.

I have given each section an introduction by way of summary and comment, except the first and last. The first consists of quotations that bear directly on the entire theme: they add up to a general statement by the competitors of their dreams and demands, plans and proposals in the matter of their ideal school. I regard it as a sort of opening fanfare. It is stirring enough, I believe, to be thought of in such terms.

Two final words. The first is to anyone who may be unaccustomed to children's writing. There is nothing here that must be apologized for and much that is extraordinarily well expressed. (It is interesting to note, incidentally, how many of the best entries are in verse). Here and there, however, a boy or girl uses that very heavy prose that is peculiar to adolescence, and under which, for any reader unfamiliar with such writing, the force of the ideas and even the sincerity itself may be lost. The prose used by some adolescents is heavy only because they believe that no idea can have weight unless it is expressed in the most ponderous phrases available. It is a kind of literary puppy fat and must be allowed for.

My other last word is addressed to anyone inclined to suspect that the editor chose to quote entries that supported his own views on schooling in Britain today. My basis of choice was simple: I was looking for any entry, or part of an entry, that seemed to me intelligent, interesting, amusing, well-expressed. It is this test, so far as I am qualified to apply it, that all the entries quoted have passed. All one can say of such unanimity of opinion as has emerged is that this is what is broadly felt by children who are intelligent, interesting, amusing, and express themselves well.

The Key to Life is Flexibility

The school I would like would be perfect, glorious in every
way, where you wouldn't worry yourself to death over things,
wouldn't get bored, and yet wouldn't get lethargic. It would be a
friendly school, everyone familiar with everyone, everyone
co-operative, with ambitions, big ideas for the future.

Gillian, 13

My basic criticism of school is that pupils don't like it.

The infant and primary schools are considered unimportant
(compared to other ages), and so school is allowed to be interesting.
As we get older our school life becomes less and less interesting as
our teachers attempt to cram us with as much knowledge as possible for the exams. He passes or fails it – and forgets all about it.
Exams are good as objective methods of finding how much one
knows, but there is more to life than exams.

Apparently a boy is not supposed to have any natural curiosity
for school subjects, and the way they are taught it is quite true.
Attempts to induce learning by prizes, stars, etc., fail because
learning is not competitive.

Teaching machines can be put to good use, but indiscriminate
use makes them boring and ignored. For some things a teacher is
indispensable. A teacher may also introduce discussion and
humour, although more often than not we laugh at, and not with,
him.

I object to corporal punishment, but even more to the casual
clouts handed out for reasons as unfair as a teacher's anxiety or for
a pupil just not understanding. Corporal punishment is brutal and
degrading. We boys are thinking, often mature, human beings. I
have seen a teacher hit a boy hard and say, 'Don't bully!' – it
will only make him bully more. The learning induced by it will
be quickly forgotten, and the subjects hated evermore. Moreover,
with better-adjusted teachers we become unmanageable as a sort
of recompense, and they, too, may resort to corporal punishment.
It also produces senseless flouting of school rules.

The pitiful thing is that the prefects have now forgotten the lower-form boy's point of view and punish him as they were punished.

As for the number of senseless rules made up by the school – we ignore them. This brings risk of ignoring sensible rules.

My main complaint is that we have so little say in school affairs. Naturally the boys who are allowed most say are those who have conformed to school ideals and regulations. Most boys just ignore our 'school duty' and when ordered to pick up litter for the glory of the school, just sit down and pick daisies. We are all expected to be devoutly religious, and atheism is in no way recognized. While one can complain at a serious offence, there is no defence for a boy 'picked on' by a teacher.

On the whole there is less need for radical changes in school organization – it makes little difference if lessons are held under a tree or in a skyscraper. It appears large schools are inevitable, but anonymity could be dispelled by good teacher–boy–parent relations (if possible informal). Widened horizons are provided by athletic 'houses', with chances for boys of all specialities to mix.

I believe in co-educational schools because life is co-educational.

Maths has always been taught so drearily, especially when it is so important. Some pupils are even set long sums as punishment!

To sum up – the average boy goes to school, becomes bored, gets into mischief, is punished, 'takes it out' on other boys, is crammed with knowledge for the exams, passes or fails his exams, forgets and has learnt to hate that subject through bad teaching.

The average teacher (even the idealistic sort) has to force much knowledge on boys, tries teaching without punishment, boys 'take it out' on him for the vicious masters, he becomes a vicious master.

So, basically, make the subject a joy to learn, interesting and worthwhile; cut out force; give us a say in the school.

You must remember that I have discounted all the friendliness and humour of boy and teacher – but the school system tries to do this too.

There is more to school than academic results.

S. (boy), 15

At last we have been consulted. I, an average fifteen-year-old public schoolgirl, am now allowed to voice my opinion on the school that I would like to attend.

To start with, I would abolish the word 'school' from the English language. It is such an ugly word, which changes in meaning every year that you pass through the school. When I was at a pre-school age, the word seemed such an adult word, so grand and exciting. After ten years of it, the word is childish, young and dull. Instead the school should be called a college.

Judith, 15

Give me the school where discipline, regimentation and good manners are *not* everything. We would rather have a school where we can talk on equal terms with our teachers on sex, morals, ethics, royalty, religion, etc. We want the school where teaching will be equated with a perpetual quest for *truth, beauty, integrity*. A school where personality and brain-building come first and diplomas or certificates last. After all, a diploma or degree is not the perfect vaccine against stupidity.

Cosette, 17

Is life divided up into sections? No, I say.
Then why have subjects at school?
Teach living at school,
And living means understanding,
And understanding is all.

Therefore I say throw out your timetables,
Throw away your rulers and bring in teachers.
Comprehensives without rules and streams and exams (one way),
Comprehensives with laughter and learning and communications
(two way).
That's what I want man,
But it costs bread and that's needed for our next nuclear
submarine.

The key to life is flexibility
Then you can breathe
Not suffocate
And die

Don't get panarchy
I don't want anarchy
Just sympathy
For the pimply.

Paul, 17

... **most of all, Lord,** let those in authority realize that we are human beings, with brains and minds capable of acting without prompting, not computers to be programmed and switched on and off.

Anne, 17

Dear Welfare State,
It is ironic that such a harmonious relationship as ours should be thrown into confusion over the matter of my education. Perhaps I should make my ideas clear to you....

Primarily the school is a body of people, and not a building. In my school there would be a healthy mixture of athletes and intellectuals, of races and creeds. At last you allow the social classes to work together, but how rigidly you separate the scientist, the linguist and the artist....

My ideal school also provides a wide and varied education. Nothing disheartens more than a subject one detests and is made to study. The pupil slaving uninterestedly at his desk must be so close to whole realms of fascinating subjects waiting to enthrall him, but a passport is never granted because of a limited syllabus and an understaffed school. I cannot impress upon you too greatly how vital unharassed and enthusiastic teachers are. There is no substitute for the infectious human element, the teacher deeply in love with his subject. He alone will set fire to my soul. I need guidance to mould my chalky dreams into a rich and satisfying adulthood. My need is now, today. Tomorrow is someone else. Teach me not to be apathetic, share your wisdom, listen to my ideals.

Susan, 16

... if it were run smoothly and efficiently, I should not care whether my school were grammar, comprehensive or secondary modern, as long as I was happy in it. If any school can produce this effect on a pupil, I think it could consider itself a success for this reason alone, although good examination results would probably follow as a by-product. I hope that many of such schools will exist in the near future, and if one has already come into being, I take off my hat to it.

Sharon, 15

I consider it essential that the school should change with the body of pupils it contains and with the society in which they must be adapted to live.

Lesley, 17

I don't think I would get on very well in my ideal school because I am too used to being told what to do.

Frances, 15

Our school is like a sausage machine.

Churn, churn, churn – and there we have it, an eight-O-levelled genius. Three cheers for the G.C.E. and this product of the examination system : a stuffed puppet, reeling off facts and dates and predigested ideas at the pull of a string, wondering if it was worth it and if this really is intelligence.

Boredom. Twenty-eight pairs of vacant eyes regarding with a hollow stare the woman at the front of the room who does the churning. Twenty-eight minds, too apathetic to think, and twenty-eight bodies, too lethargic to do anything except sprawl over desks and carve names, with infinite care, on the lids.

This is education. This is the way in which a child's enthusiasm for learning is quelled to a point of non-existence. Is it surprising that so many people escape after O-level, the climax of the whole ludicrous system?

I am not educated in the sense that I can hold my own in adult society. I have felt continually suppressed at school, and any confidence I gained has been thwarted. Much more emphasis should be laid on oral self-expression. It is not easy to bring a shy, self-conscious child out of his or her shell, but the effort should be made. It is difficult to imagine what hell a self-conscious child can go through, longing to express himself yet finding the effort too great and too painful. Much potential is lost, and many children come to hate school simply because it is a place where they cannot bring themselves to discuss their ideas and emotions....

Mine are no highly impossible dreams.... Once the fundamental difficulties are overcome, schooldays could well become the best days of one's life, the old sick myth becoming a reality and not merely a saying at which schoolchildren themselves instinctively cringe.

Elizabeth, 16

Step with me into a future school.
I'll show you around.
Even at a glance you've found
Things very different and strange.
    – Where are the clouds of white dust
    From scraping chalk?
    Nobody sits on wooden chairs, at wooden desks,
    Listening to teachers talk.
    The framed blackboard is nowhere to be seen.
    Everything is clean.
    The rooms are bright,
    And large, and wide, and very light.

No one minds what we wear.
Clothes aren't considered important,
So usually our feet are bare.
No one minds about anything much, really.
    – There is no whisper
    Of engraved desks, arranged in ranks,
    Or uniforms.
    How could you bear
    The drabness? Didn't you care
    That each child was an echo
    Of his neighbour?

We study at school for three days each week.
For the last hour of the third day
We hold discussions, in groups.
We talk on many things,
From religion to politics,
To our own personal problems.
We discuss human relationships,
And we look back, and see
What happened when knowledge gave man power.
Then we realize the importance
Of wisdom, as well.
     – These discussions are led
     By a student who is studying
     For A.O.E.s.
     (Those are the Advanced Oral Exams.
     When a pupil has taken one,
     He writes a thesis on their improvement.
     Not many people are bright enough
     To take them all. I won't be.
     You have to be really clever, you see.)

It is a good school.
Hard work, sometimes,
But people always lend
A hand.
I can depend on someone
To help me understand.
There is so much to learn
That I will only touch the edge of it –
And simply sift the sand.
     – If I had a good brain
     I would dig really deep, and learn.
     But I am not shaped for that.
     I have as much to give
     As the bright ones.
     I know how to live
     Even if I never reach second in command.
     I have my purpose, too
     If we were all brilliant,
     Who would be the crew?

There is a lot for me to do
To prepare me for whatever is in store.
But although I am a student, and I learn,
I am not preparing for life.
I am alive now.
Learning is the start of something stretching before me,
And my heart
Says it will be great.
But I can wait.
This present learning tense suits me all right,
Although I'm not too bright.

Melanie, 14

Extract from 'Talks for Students: the Anatomy of Power'.
The Rt Hon. Paul Dean, Prime Minister, reminisces:

Interviewer ... and it was in the year after this, 1989, was it not,
that you were invited to become Minister of
Education in Harvey's Labour Ministry?

Minister Yes, and I won't pretend that it was not without
considerable trepidation that I accepted the post. It
was at that time that the experimental phase of
education had begun to break down, initially because
of the inherent lack of conformity over the country
as a whole. Yet this was really only a symptom of the
collapse; one felt at the time that the real cause
was that education and society had somehow got out
of step. As is well known, I have never seen education
as a separate entity; for instance, when you and I
were at school the 'full examination' system, with its
eleven-plus, O-level, A-level and degree-level
examinations, was attuned to a competitive and
technological environment where employers needed
a code of reference that could be applied to their own
labour needs. When our technology, and as a direct
consequence, our industry reached that advanced

level where it rendered the men who had called it into existence mere anachronisms, technological education, or the 'career training' of the sixties, had no more relevance. There was no technology that men could tamper with; there were no more careers. The whole system had to be re-thought....

It had become apparent then that it was becoming rapidly less necessary for us to work in an economic sense; our problem was to be in the use of 'leisure time'. Here, of course, we were probably a little slow to adjust to the new situation, although it had been foreseen by a number of writers and economists.

Interviewer You were trying to fill this 'leisure time'?

Minister Well, that is a somewhat clinical way of expressing it. We believed that while man's capabilities in the field of science had been greatly exceeded, the arts had been neglected. Perhaps even calling them the 'Arts' lays me open to the charge of being somewhat reactionary. But we recognized the need to be creative.

Interviewer How did you try to implement this?

Minister I have never been addicted to 'forms of government' in education; I have always believed that a good teacher would succeed whatever system he was working in. And, of course, the 1972 Education Act abolishing the public schools, coupled with the widespread under-employment caused by automation, gave us a very large pool of suitable manpower. We had to have a system, of course, and for expediency we drew up the 1989 Education Act, whereby the comprehensive system, tried as long ago as 1965, I believe, was made mandatory. We were helped in our efforts by the increasing disuse of the old examinations as qualifications became irrelevant. We had to bring 'order out of chaos', I like to think, and our system allowed us to use the profusion of buildings erected during the hotch-potch period after 1968. I remember writing a memorandum in November 1987 defining what subjects should be taught. I broadly described them as literature, art, music, philosophy, history and sport, but in real terms it just meant leading the children to an understanding of an artistic discipline which would be relevant to their future leisure.

Interviewer   You described it then as 'teaching people to live'.

Minister   I am not very proud of that phrase; it suggests the sixties idea that if you taught children to drive, or to cook, you were training them for life. We tried to take the facets of school life : drama, school plays, games, which we had enjoyed, and to apply similar techniques in other arts subjects, literature and history for example. We did not perpetuate the system of children 'doing Shakespeare' as if for an examination; we tried first to encourage the children to write creatively, then show them creative writing, for example. If a child has an affinity for literature, that is the direction in which he can expand his mind by writing or reading; for participating as an audience is obviously a very important way of thinking creatively.

Interviewer   Of course there was some opposition to your plans?

Minister   Yes, a great deal of very bitter criticism that I can only attribute to. . . .

John, 17

They enter through glass, automatically opening,
To an atmosphere controlled and pleasant.
Thoughtlessly, they press buttons and pull knobs :

26

They are absorbed in work,
And they learn.

They learn to adapt themselves to life which lies ahead;
Computers are routine, even friendly.
Theirs is a technological wonderworld, yet
Still nature is to them
A wonder.

There will be no classrooms in their schools, no bells to interrupt.
They will never shrink from the dreaded thoughts
Of exams : exams for them will not exist.
They have ability
To excel.

If only their life could be ours (the time is too soon).
They are futuristic things alone.
We remain in the present, and in the past
Which catches up with us,
Unfairly.

Johanna, 15

Preserve us from the insularity of small, ancient grammar schools, which churn out more sportsmen than scholars, and consider science to be a new-fangled notion which will soon be forgotten. Let us be taught for the future, not for the past. Let us both work and play. Let there be no distinction arising from a few hours' work, done by frightened children who find an end to life when life should just be beginning. Oh Lord : abolish the eleven plus.

Anne, 17

My ideal school would be run on the lines of the present university system. There would be no classrooms but lecture theatres; after each lecture the students would have to attend a discussion group consisting of a teacher and five students. In this discussion group they would discuss the ideas put over in the lecture. It would not be compulsory to attend the lectures, but would be compulsory to go to the discussion groups. The whole school would be run by a team of non-teaching managers whose sole job would be to look after the administrative side of the school. They would organize such things as timetables and registers. In doing this they would free teachers from such jobs as looking after school meals and handing out books.

T. (boy), 16

My conception of an ideal school is a co-educational day-school. I see no advantage to be gained through cutting children off from their parents and, often, from all outside affairs for most of the year through boarding school, nor in segregating the sexes. Schools, after all, are not only to educate but also to fit the pupil for his life ahead, so that boarding and segregated schools which often cause social upsets and shyness are a bad idea. It is argued that a boarding school teaches the pupil to 'stand on his own two feet' and to live in a community, but, in my opinion, ordinary day school will do that equally well. The child has to defend himself and be independent just as much, but for shorter periods of time, which is an advantage for a sensitive person.

Alexandra, 13

Youth clubs, dances, shows, societies, dramatic clubs, cinemas, etc., in the school, held frequently, could turn it into a place of friendship and happiness, rather than dread.

Lietta, 12

The school I would like to go to,
Existing in my head,
Would be better than other schools;
For the work I would have to do
Would be to carry around
The cracking head I own.
I would not need to assume a facade...
I would be an umbrella man;

Re-covering twisted ribs
With black self-knowledge.
Knowing I cannot fly I would still want to fly.

I cannot go to my school,
But must learn to live in your word-covered world
And learn about your things.
Calling a leaf green instead of looking;
And never knowing that in your lives you had Auschwitz...
What can I do but live
When I leave your school?
Sitting at a dead desk
I will forget
What I mean...

David, 15

When we look at our schools today and politicians say we've got one of the best educational systems in the world, we realize how low standards must be.

Why do we go to school? Do we go to learn what two and two add up to? Do we go to learn how to play netball? Is not the idea of going to school to learn to 'get on' with other people, to learn to share and help, to learn to enjoy and to be stimulated and satisfied? Surely getting a detention for speaking is not helping towards these things? In the school I would like, the relationship between teacher and pupil would be changed. Instead of the teacher *telling* the pupil, both teacher and pupil would learn together, creating warm relationships, clear understanding and a zest for knowledge. We *know* that anyone, if treated as a human being and not bawled at for dropping a ruler, etc., can get on and will.

For good academic standards to exist there must be a will to learn. In the majority of schools today there is no will to learn, and that is why many children wish to leave school early....

The pupils would have great freedom, restrictions would be minimized. If a pupil wished to stay on to work or play, that pupil would be permitted to. The school need not be lavish, though pleasant surroundings would help everyone to be happier. With a small amount of money and a large amount of care, the school could be a place which was loved by everyone.

In this type of school, free expression, free thought, freedom to work at one's own pace would exist. In this school, hours would pass pleasantly, 'lessons' would not exist because the pupils would have time to find out why, when and how.

The pupils would talk freely about religion, politics, music, sport or whatever else they would wish to discuss. They would quietly (or loudly) debate, read and laugh. It would be a place where the pupils would be learning to live with each other and with 'outsiders', i.e. teachers; also a place for reasoning, cogitating, studying about things of importance to mankind.

Who knows – perhaps among the pupils of Britain one would turn out to be an inventor of a method for feeding the starving. . . .

This is a school! A place where people together learn to live together and love one another, where people learn to reason, learn to understand and above all learn to think for themselves. School was not invented just for the little people to become the same as the big people, but for the pupils to learn how to live and let live. Money is not what is needed so much as common sense, and the school I would like – in fact, the school I long for – would be a thing of the present. *Now!*

Judith, 13

My school would play a dual role, preparing its pupils for both citizenship and examinations in the morning and afternoon, and becoming a centre for community life in the evenings and holidays. This would engender a purposeful, happy society, not mesmerized by technological progress but resolved to harness it for the benefit of all men.

The economic argument for the greater utilization of school facilities is compelling, for at present they are only being used at fifty per cent of their capacity. The country's money is being criminally wasted, duplicating these existing facilities. . . . With a resurgence of interest in community life, a school offering its facilities to the public would soon become the pivot of that locality, much as the church was in the Middle Ages. Then, with people meeting and exchanging ideas and opinions, the barriers of prejudice, class and age would begin to erode, and children and adults alike would be taught citizenship by example. Thus the school would become the hub of community life, resulting in ex-pupils not regarding school as a closed chapter in their lives but a preparation for the world, and so in their turn giving advice to succeeding years of pupils.

David, 16

School, 2000 A.D.

My school's red brick, complete with clock tower,
Rugger in London clay, and starched white collars;
Ancient uncomfortable desks, splinters and dust.
Yet how do I see the school of the future?

A computer lies obsolete in the corner,
Good only for last year's curriculum:
But now a robot master plugs itself in
To obtain facts which it must pass on.
A siren warns the form that class begins.
The boys lie in anthropomorphic chairs,
Ease on their earphones and listen to
The toneless voice of the robot.
Briefed from the master robot he poses a question:
'The constituents of a clathrode compound?'
Electrically operated plastic arms
Elevate above the polyether chairs
To signify they know the answer,
And boys mumble answers into their crystal mikes.

The lesson drones on ... then a gay cascade
Of electronic sounds informs it's lunch time.
Down to the Feeding Hall by mono-rail they speed,
A sunlit room floating in space ...
Boys stand before vast shining machines;
Press-button feeding is the rule of the day.
This one gives shepherd's pie, this treacle stodge,
Eaten from paper plates, disposable.

Then to the gym, for trampolines in space or
Half an hour's horseplay in the low gravity chamber.

This is the school I'd like to go to ... I think?

C. (boy), 13

No Watery cabbage, milk pudding, lakes of custard, compulsory Latin or P.T., art or music exams, teachers' gowns, homework, school hats.
Yes Practical hints on shopping, entertaining, etc., and clothes that suit us, more films and television programmes, more projects and plays in class, more visits to concerts, etc. *Discussion of all types of art and music: pop, jazz, light and serious classical music.* Decent dinners (if possible), earlier dismissals, variety of sports at P.T., French that means something, i.e. commercial, letter-writing, etc., and not (*true*): 'The soldiers are guarding the hotel where the actress is arriving with her niece in their big car.'

Elizabeth, 11

My ideal school would be comprehensive. This system has many advantages and probably best prepares young people to face life in this modern world. I am a pupil in such a school and I am happy in it, working my way into higher sets as comprehensive education far-sightedly allows. Children from all walks of life mix, and this helps them to understand the way in which richer or poorer people live.

Sheila, 15

The school I like is a mordern comprehensive.*
I have been fortunate to attened a College where my parents paid for my tution, at this College on my first term I had very keen Masters to me, they seemed to have been of the Unvesity trained type and were keen to teach and encourage one but for some reasons unknown to me, these kind teachers dissap-

---

* I have retained the original spelling here because it seems to me to add to the meaning of a very moving piece of writing.

pered from the scene and I was left in the hands of others who were unable to get me to understand what they taught.

By this time my parents realized my lack of interest and I was transferred to a very modern Comprehensive school this school was built in 1958 and it is better eqiped than my former Grammer school. We have free transport to matches (football and cricket) while at my Grammer school we had to pay to attend all sports.

While there are more children in the classes at the morden comprehensive there are special trained teachers to teach the not so bright children like myself during the week. One per week we the dull children get this extra helpful tution to help us to absorb the lessons of the normal class.

I love my morden comprehensive school as it has a new well equipped science laboratory gymnasium and other useful rooms that were lacking in my former Grammer school.

Henry, 13

This, dear outsider, is the English lesson.
You will see that I drop blots of ink, to find
what shape they will become –
startling, living stars – and then, with inspired vocabulary,
I will describe their variety.

There is no conversation or fidgeting, you say?
We are engrossed, captivated by the infinity of chance.
Our teacher prompts, not chides; our interest,
is already there, only waiting to expand
with encouragement.

Bells? They never jar our train of thought!
This morning is devoted to experiment and observation;
later, we have a science lesson. 'What effect
does distance of falling have on an ink shape? Why
does a formless mass assume such linear beauty?'

Not what you are used to, I observe.
(You never enjoyed discovery of the fantasy of ink.)
Our stained fingers in turn create prints –
they are unique and beautiful.
Have you never noticed?

33

This, of course, leads us to paper – yes, paper.
We can devote our afternoon to study
of manufacturing processes, timber and Canada.
'Where is Canada?' someone says – thus
a great country is discovered, by us.

Now for craft. Let us build a logging community!
We use matchsticks and glue to create miniature cabins,
and pipecleaners become men. A waste of time?
My dear sir, all art lessons are a waste of time,
but ours are interesting.

(I hear you murmur, 'Shakespeare? Archimedes?
do you learn nothing of them?' Well, rather than follow
blindly the great masters, we discover basic theories first,
so we are fit to appreciate and understand their works.
Would you try to read without knowing the alphabet?)

So, you see, in one day we progress from ink-spots
to Canada. And we have learnt much,
because we wanted to; we work with enthusiasm,
as you may have seen. Lesson links with lesson, while
friendly teachers pilot our energy.

Equipment here is inexpensive – we believe that
a freely-encouraged mind achieves more on its own
than one pursued, hemmed in by a computered timetable.
Naturally, sir, they hold a place in modern education –
second in importance, please, to the individual.

Our teachers understand us. If indoor projects become
monotonous, we race out in the sun with balls;
or, over there, quieter ones tend the flowerbeds
(putting their ingenuity and sense of grace to use
in the serenity of nature).

School, for us, serves a purpose. We well know
we are not here to pass exams (you look surprised!)
but to learn to develop and respect ourselves
by personal achievement.

'I hear, and I forget;
I see, and I remember;
I do, and I understand.'
A Chinese proverb; which reminds me, here, to your right,
you see a wall chart on Eastern customs
which our juniors have made ...

Elizabeth, 16

There are weekly quizzes on the work, with a little healthy rivalry. Subjects are tested naturally (for example, the science test is mostly practical), and coming last has no stigma attached to it. In the video-tape classes, pupils are not streamed or graded, since groups will form naturally; not only academic groups but also those connected with spare-time activities. This 'grouping' does not give rise to envy or branding because it is not imposed by adults. Age, too, has become a lower barrier; in one classroom, boys of eighteen and girls of ten can be working on different tapes simultaneously.

The break between holidays and school has been made less sudden. School is not loathed, there is no can't-wait-for-the-holidays feeling, there are no boarding schools.

The computerized kitchen hums, the air conditioners puff. In a corner a boy lies asleep, having spent too long the night before doing experiments with timing machines, and some eight-year-olds listen attentively to a tape on Renaissance art. The key to this school? It is part of everyday life, and an enjoyable and very interesting part.

Jeremy, 16

No one would leave until eighteen. This is because I don't believe school children learn enough about people and the world.

Ruth, 13

This school would only have people like me who like writing stories and poetry and none of us would laugh at each other for

35

being odd and queer. There would be no handwork and we'd have maths without the problems and we'd have *at least* one lesson a day to make up poetry. There'd be only ten to a class and we would all have nice names like Lalage (Greek for chatterbox), Zoë (Greek for life), and Charlotte because it was the christian name of Charlotte Brontë, and Imogen from Shakespeare.

Everyone would co-operate with one another and we'd act our own adaptations of novels like *Jane Eyre*. We'd read lots of biographies about famous people like writers and musicians. Composing music for our orchestras would be as important as arithmetic, and famous people would come on unannounced visits to discuss topics of the hour. To have television in our homes would be quite unusual, and we would discuss books instead of television at the dinner table.

Teachers would be there to help and *not* to organize, and they might hint at something to do but not make us do it. They would make sure we had discovered all the important aspects of life and give us gardens to cultivate. We would go on visits to places like Kenwood House, Haworth and Blenheim Palace, and organize ghost hunts in the weekends! The murals on the classroom walls would be of the latest aspect in life we had discovered.

There would be a 'screaming room' where anyone could go and make as much noise as they wanted to without anyone hearing and objecting.

When I'm older I'll establish this place for people who feel different. There will be a severe entrance examination to see that you really suit the school, and the fees will be essays, poetry or paintings according to your talents.

Lalage, 11

My ideal school would be the first really comprehensive school in the world. In general, our schools now are very exclusive – they include only those who can gear themselves to the particular discipline of the present examination structure. Those whom my school would particularly aim to reach would be the pupils of undoubted but undeveloped ability, stifled by their hostility to the discipline and atmosphere of school. The qualities I would most want to nourish – curiosity, imagination and creativity. But the most obvious characteristic of my pupils would be, I hope, their interest and enjoyment.

Rachel, 17

My idea of a school I'd like would have understanding teachers (who are few and far between at present) who would try to understand the pupils' difficulties and not look upon the pupils as illiterate sub-humans. The pupils would also be treated as individuals and not as a flock of sheep all with the same purpose in life. ... The teachers would work in unison and not think that the maths teacher was aloof from the P.E. teacher or too proud to mix with the laboratory assistants.

The pupils would be of all nationalities and creeds: boys and girls, Jews and Moslems. This would help them in later life to have no colour prejudice and to know that one nationality or creed is no better than another.

The school (and beyond) would be a one-class society: nobody rich, nobody poor. ...

Boy, 13

... And Freedom

My finger-nails are splitting because I think too much.
But please I cannot help it when I am so hungry.
Blackboard chalk tastes of memories on my tongue
– I built a wall and pulled it down.
But we are under heaven watching frogs
Spawning. Then Yoga next when we have tired
Of hen-or-egg infinity.
Pink-grey sun pricks needles in the scalp
Of my imagination. So fetch the paints
And this one sunset will not ever die.

And in my age shall I seek in the dusts of flesh
For some sad signs on which to weep,
As grain in a cockerel's craw.
Religions now: my Humanist views expounded forth,
Ground into dirt, to rise a swelling corn

To challenge god and prejudice.
The boy telepath down there is being trained
A different way from me. He knows no maths or history:
A moron, textbooks from the past would say.
But genius knows itself with calm.
And when the willow tree bends her back to laugh,
Then walk I, purple moon, with free breath.

Jeanne, 15

I hope that all the schools of tomorrow will primarily have much more freedom and variety than those of today. By freedom I mean much more time to work individually on subjects or aspects of subjects the pupils find interesting; and by variety I mean more flexibility in the weekly programme of lessons.

Gillian, 14

The school I'd like is what I have: my mother teaches my brother and me at home. We study maths, English, science, history, geography, French and scripture.

This system has many advantages. The most important is that we can learn at our own speed; thus I have recently started A-level maths but am still struggling with O English, while my brother, who is three and a half years younger, is advanced in English but only average at arithmetic. Another advantage is that we have much more free time than other children; we don't waste time travelling to and fro and, as we have individual work, the education officer agreed to shorten lesson times for us. I spend a lot of my leisure time reading, bird watching, stamp and coin collecting, doing jigsaws, carpentry, painting, listening to radio, watching T.V., swimming, playing chess, draughts, tennis and table tennis. Another advantage is that we are not hedged in by a lot of silly rules and regulations. We are also free from bullying big boys and from pressure to start bad habits like smoking and drug taking. We dress in comfortable, sensible clothes and do not have to wear some ridiculous uniform, nor do we have to play compulsory games. Again, we have home cooking all the time.

When my mother started, a lot of people told her she was foolish because we would never learn to mix. I don't think this is true because, although I've always liked some time by myself, my brother likes and has lots of friends with whom he goes to play and who come and play with him. ... It was also said that we would grow up selfish : I hope we're not. About once a fortnight we have a stall in our front garden to aid Oxfam and have collected £4 2s 3d so far this year. We also do a few odd jobs around the house. People also said Mother would find it too much. I know we get her down at times, but she survives and looks, so people say, much younger than she is. ...

The only disadvantage of the system to my mind is the difficulty of doing much advanced practical work in science because of the amount of apparatus required. ...

I think it would solve a lot of problems if more people followed our system. Of course, not everyone is qualified to teach older children, but millions of mums could teach juniors. This would reduce the terrible overcrowding in some primary schools. Again, as children would be home for longer, it might help to decrease the birth rate.

Frank, 12

Perhaps in the not-so-distant future, man's intelligence will have improved so much that children will be able to be taught by their parents in the home.

Jennifer, 13

'The roots of education are bitter, but the fruit is sweet,' wrote Aristotle; but need these roots be so unpalatable? When learning ceases to be looked upon by the majority of schoolchildren as a chore, but instead as a sequence of processes just as enjoyable, and more fulfilling, than their normal out-of-school activities, then our educational system will have justified itself. After all, education is *not* an entirety in itself, wrapped up tightly and isolated in protective cloth. It is *not* just another necessary facet of child development. Schools must allow pupils to recognize them for what they are (or should be) – a means for gaining access

to and absorbing all the exciting and stimulating things that sur-
round them.

The school I would like to see would strive to cater not for
artificial ends such as examinations (which are frequently tests of
what one knows, not *how* this knowledge has been gained and to
what advantage), but instead treat the artistic and scientific ful-
filment of the largest number of pupils as an end in itself.

Kenneth, 17

The ideal school is united mankind :
Easy to talk of, far harder to find –
A scattered-out spring which takes ages to wind.

Our sparkling dreams are spacious and broad,
With acres of land laid out fit for a lord;
But the schools we would like we cannot afford.

The schools we would like are not crowded or damp,
Don't ruin our eyes with a single dim lamp,
And seem from outside like a flood-victim camp. ....

The schools that I want are not built for display,
Concealing within them dead customs of clay,
Entombing ideals which have long had their day.

The measure of schools rests in people, not bricks;
Depends on discovery, not drilled in with sticks;
No vast ocean windows can make people mix.

All the cracking of slums is only a start,
And even the noble 'Less testing, more Art'
Will not give the arrogant a quick change of heart.

The school that I want is more than mixed sexes,
With learning a game, winning nice golden 'x's;
But 'How do I get it?' – that always perplexes. ....

David, 17

I must dismiss my dream for some fortunate, lucky child in a dream world, while I face the enjoyable hardships of school to-morrow.

Gillian, 13

Dark Relics that Our Age is Afraid to Demolish

It was school buildings, with teaching machines, that really brought out the sense of fantasy in these children. Having none of the problems of an actual architect, they let themselves go, and there can't for a very long time have been such a lavish decreeing of pleasure-domes. In respect of the wilder notions, I have felt it necessary to be the man from Porlock : I have cut most of those visions short, and few of them are represented here. It is pleasant to think of schools like ziggurats, with lifts and sliding roofs and amazing bunches of domes; schools capable of moving to Africa, under their own steam (or electronic power) when the geography lessons reached that point; or buildings based on some outlandish geometrical shape. But I was reminded of the story of the parson who prayed for rain during a drought, and was instantly answered by a sensational downpour. 'Thank you, Lord,' he murmured, 'but we should welcome a sense of proportion.'

And yet even the fantasticating, it seems to me, is making a point. As they look in other areas of education for more excitement than they have now, so in this matter of buildings. The domes, the curiously much-favoured round schools were reactions against a quality in school buildings that many inveigh against : their *squareness*. I think I understand this. The children are saying what some of their elders say when they grumble about the box-like quality of so many houses. An assemblage of box shapes, and most schools of any period are that, rarely provides any sense of mystery, or has a romantic quality. Children, most of whom are quite naturally enormously romantic, would like their daily environment to have some devious and unobvious characteristics. Almost certainly, we fail to take even cautious note of this need in them when we build those usually very rational and four-square schools of ours.

They cry out for colour, and are very conscious of the drab uniformity of many of the walls within which they sit. They would like to have some say at least in the ephemeral decoration of their schools. They long for attractive grounds, and especially for trees. 'We *do* notice,' says one girl; and one is reminded of the statement that sometimes the best of teachers makes, that the school building doesn't matter. The roots of such a statement are obvious enough; a great many of our school buildings aren't even remotely enjoyable, and a teacher aware of this may feel a very real need to point out that a school can be a good one despite this seediness of its setting. And indeed it can : and if one had to make a choice, one would choose bad buildings and good teachers rather than bad teachers and a palace. Yet it is clear to me, especially since I have always taught in buildings of a fairly monstrous character, that buildings do matter; that the fabric of a school does speak to the children, and that it says, 'I express the community's notion of what you are worth, of the environment you deserve.' An ugly, inconvenient, wholly unpleasing school building makes a daily statement to the children; and children *do* notice. It is perhaps hardly news that a great many of these essays either referred directly to buildings of such gracelessness, in which the writers found themselves, or did so indirectly, by the wistful or extravagant visions they expressed.

But after all the wild dreams, we are left with a residue of very reasonable wishes. Not only for that touch of architectural imagination, but also for comfort. Hundreds of children mentioned air conditioning. Schools are so often too hot or too cold. They would like, especially in some areas of a school, more soundproofing. They don't for the life of them see why school furniture is so often made for dwarfs, or why it should be so squarely uncomfortable. The boy who is quoted here as saying he doesn't want armchairs, but would at least welcome a chair with a comfortable back, is speaking for hundreds among the essayists – millions of children altogether, I would guess, remembering how unjust I would feel when I complained of fidgeting by boys who had sat all day on hard wooden seats. The children suspect, quite rightly I imagine, that they have such tough and uneasy furniture because the authorities fear that anything more considerately constructed might have a short life. Again this is a sphere in which the children claim that if they are trusted, if they are given responsibility for something worth having, then that trust will not be misplaced. I am with them here. I do believe that, on the whole, careless treatment of school buildings and furniture is a response to the miserably uninteresting character of both. But the real case for improvement ought perhaps to rest on other grounds. Fair comfort is necessary for any workman; and conventional buildings and furniture form part of that generally unhelpful image of the school, as a place of rigid habits designed for the accommodation of docile dwarfs. In an important way, a fairly sophisticated building and generous furniture would help young people to relax, to feel a proper sense of importance; it would help to satisfy that longing that runs through all their essays, to be regarded as people nearing maturity.

The demand for commonrooms – rooms in which they could be at ease, be noisy or quiet, read or talk informally – came from all sides, and was clearly prompted by the same longing. The school which is square and conventional, consisting only of rooms in which to work and corridors in which to circulate, is for 'children', in the old unhelpful style. The building touched with imagination, in which there is accommodation not only for leisure but also for that important by-product of school work that lies in informal discussion and unscheduled private study – that would be a school for near adults.

Hardly a school at all, in the almost derogatory sense that so many of them find in the word. I remember an occasion when the school in which I taught was to be enlarged, and I obtained permission to hang the architect's drawings in the library. A boy stood at my elbow, looking at one of those ideal sketches in which quiet groups of pupils, twos and threes, were scattered at their ease down a vista of walks and patios, with actual trees visible at various points. 'Sir,' said my companion, 'that ain't a school. That's a *college*.'

The very sight of the old, red-bricked schools, with tiled walls and big ugly blackboards, could never inspire anyone to learn.

Peter, 15

As the earlier part of one's life revolves round school, it should be something beautiful to revolve around. All too often the schools of today are stark, unimaginative buildings, poorly constructed and, to hundreds of pairs of sleepy eyes on Monday morning, utterly depressing. Their small area of formal grounds and the playing field – if they have one – look like the aftermath of a hurricane in which are left bald patches of grass, a few scrubby bushes and one or two wind-blasted roses. It does not seem to be the done thing to have trees around.

Jane, 15

The atmosphere of a school makes a huge difference to a pupil. I recently went into a school where, as soon as I stepped in, I felt depressed. The long, low, dark corridors pressed down on me. The classrooms were so ordinary. How different would be a school with large light corridors. A classroom should be definitely *not square*. Gay, unusual curtain material at large windows makes such a difference. We do notice light shades, too, and the colour of the paintwork. Small, crowded classrooms can be depressing as well as stuffy, just as a large one seems to be full of echoes and footsteps.

Nina, 14

Dear Lord, please give us a school which is cool in summer, yet warm enough in winter for us to sit without coats and gloves. Let there be an end to these dreary places where the sun never penetrates, where only one small window opens, though the rest admit small gales, where the draughts howl through the sacred portals, and where the electric light is on, constantly, from November till April, and frequently during the rest of the year. And might we have lavatories which do not freeze up in cold weather?

Anne, 17

It is out of date in appearance (if we mention this idea, the headmaster dismisses it by saying that the board of governors would not agree to a grant for a new building, and that extensive improvement would cost too much). In winter the central heating has proved to be inadequate, and in spite of certain rooms being decorated, recently, many rooms remain in a disgusting state (old, misused desks among other things).

I end this script on a dramatic note: our school needs to be removed from the face of this earth before we are disgraced any further, and I would like to see a modern building erected on my specifications.

Alan, 16

It's an old school as they go: the four giant Ionic columns still hold up the façade. The entrance hall is decorated with wooden panels, disclosing to all who care to look the names of those who have distinguished themselves (academically) at 'Oxbridge'. The prefects wear gowns. The headmaster is a mumbling character and a B.A. The vice-principal is a jolly personage and an M.A. and a B.Litt. There aren't any proper washing facilities and the dining hall is ill-ventilated. It's all totally overwhelming and almost incredible that such tradition has survived these many years.

Peter, 16

It's all very odd. We have a brand-new language laboratory, with a film-projector affair which shows cartoons with French commentary on a T.V. screen, but our textbooks are falling to pieces. We have several large science laboratories that are clean enough to perform brain-surgery in, while our lavatories are usually minus chains or minus doorlocks or minus toilet-paper or minus all three.

Elen, 14

My own school was a number of years ago promised by the local education committee a few shelves to cope with the ever-increasing number of books in our library. The permission has been granted, but even after several years of expectant waiting the shelves have still not materialized. This may be a rather trivial matter, but I am positive that it is only a scaled-down version of many problems that are apparent in our schooling system today and that fully justify my accusations.

Patrick, 14

Deliver us from private study periods, or rather let there be some system whereby we can be alone to study – not herded into the fifteen by twelve cubbyhole (den of the school secretary until a larger room was found for her) which contains fifteen sixth formers and their desks only by dint of elaborate, tight packing. There is no blackboard, since we can find no way of preventing it falling from the mantelpiece – we have no room for an easel. Neither is there a teacher's desk. There is a chair, set at right angles to the block of desks, which remains in the room simply because it is too tightly wedged for us to manoeuvre it out. Most staff find it easiest to stand. This arrangement, further complicated by the first form, who consider it their right to use the room as a corridor, leads to most of our work being done at home, our recreation being taken in our private study time, much to the annoyance of the staff.

Anne, 17

Children live in synthetic fibre houses and then have to spend half their lives in dark relics that our age is afraid to demolish because of the loss of a grasp with the past. Children have changed, the schools should! A school should be filled with the amenities and inventions of our century. It should teach children more about the future and less about the past.

Lynda, 16

My ideal school should have ultra-modern buildings, like Liverpool's Roman Catholic cathedral, and the classrooms should be large, airy, and painted in bright colours; nothing is more depressing than dirty whites and dull greys. Too much glass is a mistake; in summer we ripen like tomatoes in a greenhouse!

Sheila, 15

The school would be a large spacious building, with underfloor central heating so that people who enjoyed going without their shoes could do so, if they wished, in comfort. The interior of the building would be decorated by the pupils of the school, as it is they who have to live amongst it.

Angela, 15

The first thing that strikes one about the school building is that it is round. This is because a circle has the smallest perimeter for its size. As there are no sharp corners, no pupil would waste his or her time, or the teachers', by vaguely gazing out of the window. The corridors are also circular, and if possible the pupils should only be allowed to go around one way (clockwise or anticlockwise) to stop struggles and squeezes.

Antony, 13 and Christopher, 13

The school I would like to attend would have to be modern in design and outlook. The quality of decoration, lay-out and furniture (plus the responsibility for these given to the students) would be so good that vandalism would be at a minimum.

Alan, 16

Through experience I know that sitting in the unbearable heat of the classroom in the summer makes one languid and unwilling to do work of any kind. Therefore it would be a great relief if we could have air conditioners in the classrooms.

Anne, 15

I can work much better in a large airy room at a pleasant temperature than in a poky ill-lit furnace!

R. (boy), 11

Three features of this school that would immediately strike a visitor comparing it with my present school would be: (a) comfort, (b) little noise, (c) efficient central heating and air conditioning. These conditions are, I believe, necessary for the most efficient, year-round learning. They also help to make it into a place where children want to go and learn, instead of making it into their anathema.

Ian, 16

Above all, education should be exciting. No educated person can claim boredom amidst so much knowledge. School life should be crammed with interest – the buildings too. Yet nothing is more depressing than the average buff-coloured classroom! Revolution must break out, the classroom must be invaded by novel colour schemes and different architectural styles, taken over by paintings and sculptures. No two should look the same. The pupils should have more freedom in the planning and execution of form room decoration and gardening. Excitement should be injected into school, so that one is completely surrounded by and part of it.

Ann, 18

Even a slight rearrangement of the room might stir a thought or two. When a shop wants to attract customers, they put on a bright and attractive display. Why couldn't this idea be used in school?

Peter, 15

Instead of rows of little square classrooms with rows of little square desks in them, there should be seven or eight large halls. Then you could divide these into soundproof, air-conditioned glass sections, or just leave it as a large hall. Then you could take one or two partitions away to make larger rooms.

Stephen, 13

Classrooms should be soundproof, so that if a maths lesson is going on on top of the music rooms, each lesson will not be distracted. It could leave disastrous results: $166532 \times 695 =$ Beethoven.

Lietta, 12

Use should be made of bright materials and paints, and form rooms should reflect the over-riding character of that form, instead of the uniform character of the actual room and the basic furniture.

Sheila, 15

The furniture in my ideal school would be designed to suit the present generation of king-size children instead of, as at present, for the midgets of yesteryear. A little comfort wouldn't come amiss, either.

Katherine, 12

Wooden chairs! They're so uncomfortable! Couldn't we have some easy chairs, not deep armchairs but just comfortable-backed chairs? The desks aren't much better, it's very painful to scrape one's knees on the bottom of them and worse still to knock one's hips against the edge.

Anne, 14

More space instead of being cramped in about 1 sq. yd of hard wood.

Angela, 13

... tables would replace desks, which are small and an enemy of knees.

Judith, 15

There are always complaints about people marking or destroying school furniture, but I think that if the school furniture was more attractive they would not want to mark or destroy it. But when most of the desks and chairs are all brown, the floor wooden, and the walls are brown and dirty grey, and people are always on about writing on desks and walls when you probably haven't touched them, it isn't easy to enjoy the lessons.

Carole, 14

Classrooms will be very different. In fact, recesses would be a better name for them. They would lead directly off the corridor with a sliding partition providing privacy when required, as in an examination. When this partition is down it will look part of the wall. These classrooms will be extremely modern, with teaching and adding machines, television sets, open bookshelves and perhaps a type of high chair at which the pupil could work, so saving space. Desks will not be seen in the school.

Lynda, 13

A room especially for drama is a good idea. You cannot make a successful attempt at a play in a space about three feet by nine. A drama room and interest is better than a classroom and boredom.

Jennifer, 15

To build commonrooms for everyone just for break and lunch time would be highly impractical; the only thing to do is to make the whole building pleasant to work and relax in, far removed from the small, dark, ink-bespattered dungeons of a past age.

Jeanette, 14

I believe the actual equipment should be kept to the bare minimum, but there should be raw materials in plenty. For example, in the old concept of a gymnasium, dangling ropes suggest you must climb them. Why not provide trees instead?

Judith, 18

I like plenty of space to play in at the breaks, with a variation of grass, concrete, trees and bushes.

Janet, 13

The building in which my school is housed will be light and modern, surrounded by large, unprohibited lawns and tarmac areas and not built to last for ever.

Janet, 16

I attend a school set in delightfully natural grounds. I do not fully appreciate this at my unperceptive age, but cannot help feeling proud when its beauty is drawn to my attention.

Sheila, 15

Grounds always improve the looks of a school and also, if big enough, are pleasant to walk in before or after dinner. Sometimes they are not possible, as in towns; then, I think, there should be greenhouses or at least indoor flower boxes.

Anne, 14

... learning depends on atmosphere and the teachers and pupils. If you are happy, a shack will doubtless do to be merry in; round rooms with filtered sunlight can be given a miss.

Moira, 16

Gaunt buildings, shamed by brick and harsh design,
Fade hazily into a soft mist of light,
To rise again as deep, mellow-hued stone, honeyed by the sun.
Long rambling halls merge into being, ochre-tiled, shadowy-eaved.
High arched windows, arrogant and deep, colours subdued by gold,
     violet, blue of creeping vine.
And around are trees, many tall, beautiful trees,
Rustling gently on the breeze.
Sweeps of green meadowland, bracken, furze tall and uncut,
     flushed with wild flowers.
Here and there are coverts concealing leafy arbours of rough-hewn
     stone, majestic statues,
Hygeia and Diana cloaked in misty lichens.
Stretches of open water, reed-fringed, translucent, deep, ruffled by
     the wind –
The home of wild fowl and mosquitoes in summer.
Then the campus hoves into view –
Gone the sparsely vegetated area of former years –
Now filmy forms hurl javelins and discus on buoyant turf, resilient
     green,

And run like the fox and deer that peer fearless from the brush.

Gone, too, is the yard where once were children herded in the winter months,

Snuffling and stamping in the cold like a herd of musk-ox in a snowstorm.

For the young folk now is the freedom of the woodlands to do with as they please,

A place to tumble or run wild, a pleasant classroom to learn, think and dream.

At ease with nature as were the Ancient Britons of the past –

Then placidly as my vision came, it slips away with the rising heat,

And a well-aimed kick in the ribs propels slowly forth,

Back to the dusty gloom, the echoing corridors and the noisome smell of school.

Jane, 15

What the Hell's Africa Like?

The children's verdict on the teaching that many of them receive much of the time is devastating. They are bored, they feel an immense irritation and dreariness because they are being taught at – are regarded as the passive receptacles of predigested material, much of it irrelevant. They want to discover things for themselves. Children, they point out with varying degrees of patience, want to be doing things; exploring the material of knowledge with all their senses, where that is possible : and freely discussing, among themselves and with their teachers, their feelings, their findings and the whole range of their ideas.

For a very long time it has been educationally respectable to say what these children are saying : that learning ought to be by way of doing, discovery and discussion. But not only does the rational prose in which this view is expressed in reports and papers seem hopelessly unurgent beside the vivid outbursts of these young writers; but what the children say, over and over again, makes it clear that the revolution in teaching method has barely begun to touch the secondary schools. So it is still possible for a great many of these children, from a wide variety of such schools, to be begging that they be allowed to *get out* of the dead air of the classroom – to be freed from that sterile and cramped learning situation in which the teacher, the textbook and the examination-dominated syllabus have decided what should be learnt, and how it should be learnt, and that virtually everything should be presented as a hurried intellectual abstraction. Everything, at its worst (and its most common), is reduced to a *drone*, a word the children use repeatedly. So you learn about Africa – or rather, attempts are made to teach you about it – but you never *feel* Africa, or touch an African artefact, or embark on any course of inquiry that makes Africa real to you. You read about tors, but are never taken to see a tor; about dairy farms, but never visit one. But these children provide their own examples, in plenty, in the pages that follow, building up their surely unanswerable case that for a thousand purposes of learning they ought to get out of the classroom, leave behind the textbook and the blackboard and the copying of second-hand notes.

And where getting out might be of limited use, and indeed in all cases, they ask that their *imaginations* be employed. In the primary school, no one is hesitant in calling a child's imagination into play : a statement that looks cold enough beside the beautiful, glowing, wry amplification of it by the girl who four years ago in her primary school was held 'spellbound as the snake's prey' by 'the glittering eyes of the Roman gladiator', but who is now deeply depressed by droning accounts of eighteenth-century inventions. The murder of the imagination which so many of them find to be what occurs in the secondary school is one of the more striking signs of that general decline in creative and humane teaching that comes with the movement from the primary school. Facts are to be learned, the starker the better, and imagination is for the very young, and in any case there is no time now for imagination.

To be allowed to discuss and debate, not as extramural luxuries but as an intrinsic feature of learning, is another major demand. They want to talk, air their views, pit their opinions against one another; or simply, by talking, really to begin to acquire opinions. All recognize that this is incompatible with desperately crammed timetables, with the common attitudes (and perhaps the usual skills) of teachers themselves. But if children are allowed to play a greater part in the process (so one picks up their argument), then more must be learnt simply because the old pattern would be reversed in which boredom and a sense of individual insignificance are promoted by their passive role, curiosity is killed and learning cannot easily occur.

Note how they hammer the textbooks, principally because these are very often prime instruments by which the teacher makes the natural expression of curiosity – the natural making of mistakes and arguing out of issues – difficult if not impossible. The textbook is a despot, and knows all, and has already arranged the matter of learning in order (and, of course, too many teachers simply act as a kind of ventriloquist for the textbook – secondhandness added to secondhandness). The children know, by instinct sharpened by their daily impatience and boredom, that the best part of learning is the making of order for yourself.

Of course with help, from teacher and textual authority; but these should give guidance when guidance is needed, present information when information is required, and not stamp out the path from beginning to end, in advance. Is there not a deal of sense in the suggestion, made in these pages by one boy, that children should compile their own textbooks? If the suggestion is excessive, it is excessive in the right direction, surely? For what they do want, with passionate shrewdness, is to make learning their own. As another child put it, perhaps too kindly, the textbook makes no mistakes; and they see the importance of making their own mistakes.

Easy to imagine the horror of so much of the educational establishment at such ideas! Unless a severe control of material and method remains in the hands of the teacher, how shall scholarship be maintained? But the true scholar has always had to shake free from the orthodoxies of passive learning: discover how to ask his own questions: dispute with the umpteenth-hand verdicts of the textbook, shake his teacher's wits. But then, it will be asked, how shall we get everything done? If we are always leaving the classroom to 'see, feel, smell, hear, taste the subject,' going off to discover something for ourselves which, when you think of it, the teacher could assert in the form of a blackboard note in a matter of minutes; if we are constantly exercising the leisurely and wayward imagination; if we are always debating, discussing, airing views – if, indeed, discussion, so demanding of time, is to replace much of the traditional matter of teaching on the grounds that this matter might be more economically memorized by a work of reference than by a young human head; if we are not to lean on the sententious orderliness of the textbook; if we are to watch films, make wider use of libraries, cultivate breaks in routine, try out many tones and styles of speech and writing instead of learning a single style suitable for the ears and eyes of examiners; if we are going to accept such notions, all of which are put forward by children in these essays, then how on earth shall we teach all that we have to teach, all that history, geography, all the skills of punctuation, analysis, all the ages of English literature, all the mathematics and physics and chemistry, and all the languages dead and living? One answer to that question is provided by our children themselves. As things are, few of them in any meaningful sense have real hope of learning a tithe of all this. They are bored, excluded. Another answer is one many will give who have seen what a crushing chore we make of most of the education we give most of our children – such a chore as ensures that when they leave school many of them will never read a serious book again (often not even a frivolous one), or think another historical or geographical thought, or make any use of their Latin, French, German. This answer is that at the moment we not only teach our children in such a way that we crush their own natural curiosity and their desire to be, in some degree, masters of their lives, but we also teach as if everything had to be crammed into the years of schooling. We teach as if our children would drop dead the moment they left us.

The demand and the need for new teaching methods are clear enough, coming straight from the droning classroom as they do in the words of these children. They want these new methods, and the excitement of them, not for their own sakes, but because such and no others are the means by which real learning might come about. Children, because so many of them are in the middle of *not* learning, understand this.

The way forward is not so clear, given all the interest that is vested in present habits and techniques and outlooks. That the best intentions can lead to the worst results is shown by the one or two items here that give doleful accounts of new methods gone wrong. But at least the plain statement of a need might be the beginning of a plain answer.

'Now, do you all understand?' asks the frowning old maths master impatiently. Silence! 'Right then, get on with pages seventy-two to seventy-six.' The heads bow down and pens begin to scratch. A few poor boys, still not understanding, sit waiting anxiously for the bell. Others glance at the clock every few minutes. The bell goes and the tension breaks; everyone hurriedly packs his books and heaves a sigh of relief. The master walks out and the next walks in. Another forty tedious minutes. . . .

I go to a grammar school and this is a fairly accurate description of what a lot of the lessons are like. All this is wrong.

Stephen, 13

In my view, the sooner we all get out of the stuffy classroom, the better it will be for everybody. Life is much more interesting if you can go out and see something instead of just sitting in a desk and being loaded with information about it.

Lynne, 15

What a bore school is nowadays, the same as it has been for hundreds of years. What we get is the same old thing – teacher, outdated textbooks, and a class fed up to the teeth with the teacher and the school. What we need is one vast change in the educational system of this country. Children do not want to be taught at, but want to find out things for themselves. If a child is interested in the way a dogfish's heart works, let him go and find out, by cutting one up.

Robin, 16

. . . more outings during school time, field trips wherever it is possible to see the real thing, 3D education rather than flat black-and-white learning.

Anne, 18

Schools should be made better and made into a place *all* children like to go to and a place where you go because you want to go. Subjects should be made more exciting instead of sitting in a desk reading or half-listening to a teacher going on and on about a particular thing. I should like to be doing things, finding what I can do and what I can't do; not just talking about, e.g., a dairy farm but talking to the people who work there and trying to milk a cow by yourself.

Angela, 13

'What's he droning on about?' 'Africa! What the hell's that like?'

Does it look like that line of dustbins through the window? Does it feel like this inkwell? Does it sound like that traffic or this continuous drone? Does it smell like carbolic soap? Does it taste like this bubblegum?

What is the answer to this dreaming atmosphere of the classroom? There are several, but the simplest and yet overlooked one is to get rid of classrooms. Instead of stuffing children into a classroom, within four boundaries, let them get out and see, feel, smell, hear and taste the subject. Bring it alive.

Geography is the first subject that springs to mind. Almost the whole course could be held outside, in the docks, in all the types of country, by the sea and in the towns. And regularly there would be trips abroad. History too can easily be adapted, see the places where history was made, look at the old documents, dig up the churchyards, feel history.

The sciences to me cry out to get outside. Finding the chemical reactions of life, visiting factories, cyclotrons, nuclear power stations, hospitals, studying the fauna. Obviously there would be a need of laboratories where we could return and by experiment fathom out what we had observed. . . .

There would have to be a school with rooms, but furnished with soft chairs in a circle, where the classroom subjects would be taught and discussed, and where the results of the outings would be announced and discussed. There would have to be an enormous library to help us satisfy our curiosity. . . .

I say abandon classroom teaching and get out and understand things.

Richard, 15

Geography lessons are very dull. How better it would be, instead of merely accepting the fact that region A had limestone, to discover it oneself. Not to read about population distribution, but to prove it by local surveys, to see tors instead of merely reading about them.

Anne, 17

Just reading and writing about things makes it a real bore. Children lose patience very easily, and they want to be doing things all the time.

Lietta, 12

When I am older I would like to learn a bit about the job I want to take up. Work should not just be writing. Schools should vary it. In Geography I'd much prefer to go to a factory or farm than sit around discussing it. I should think the pupils would find this much more interesting and learn about it quicker, with fuller understandings. Besides, it would be a rest for the teacher.

Clare, 11

'Pupils, train your teachers!'

Johnny crashed through the garden gate and stormed down the path, demolishing some of his father's prize blooms with his trailing satchel. Finding his way blocked by the front door, he sank on to a paving stone and announced to the whole neighbourhood, 'I'ATE SCOOW!'

Johnny is by no means unique. Thousands of boys and girls throughout this country feel the same way towards this compulsory purgatory.

If Britain is to hold its own in the technological and artistic world of tomorrow, she must educate her children thoroughly and, above all, in an interesting way.

A history lesson in Johnny's school would probably go something as follows:

Lookout at the door of the classroom sees teacher approach, and tells the class to 'Belt up, it's coming!' Sudden quiet. The teacher enters. Class rises.

Teacher	Good morning, children.
Class	Good morning, sir.
Teacher	Sit down and get your exercise books out. Today I'll dictate.
Class	Oh, not again!

Teacher	Be quiet, or you'll have to stay behind tonight. Now, get your pens ready. What is it, Smith?
Johnny	Please, sir, my pen has no ink.
Teacher	Well, fill it. Had only been on the throne for a few –
Johnny	Please, sir, I didn't catch that last piece.
Teacher	Leave a space and copy it later. A few months. William, Duke of Normandy –
Johnny	Please, sir, my nib's broken.
Teacher	Stop interrupting my lesson, Smith, and stand outside the room for the rest of the period!

At the end of that lesson, Johnny would know next to nothing of the events of 1066, and after a few more lessons like that, he would lose interest in the subject, and his mind would slowly dull.

Ideally, the schools of tomorrow should keep the minds of their pupils active. The best way to accomplish this is to allow the children to take more part in the lessons. They should discuss the subject they are learning with the teacher, airing their own views and listening to other pupils'.

The atmosphere should be less formal, the teachers calling both boys and girls by their Christian names, the classes being smaller, and the lessons becoming less and less like lessons, and more like debates.

A history lesson in these circumstances would go this way:
The teacher enters and the class rises.

Teacher	Good morning.
Class	Good morning, sir.
Teacher	Now, today I thought we should leave the actual course of the Napoleonic Wars, and concentrate on Napoleon as a man. Has anyone any views on the subject?
Johnny	In the last lesson you said that Napoleon was a megalomaniac. I don't think he was.
Teacher	Can you back that up, John?
Johnny	In the first place, he didn't really want to . . . and so I don't think he was exalting himself.
Teacher	That was very interesting, John. I know there are only

> eleven of us here, but surely someone disagrees with
> what John said. What's your view, Elizabeth?

Elizabeth Well, I think that ...

I should think that a vast majority of today's school children would prefer to be taught in a school using the second method, but will probably not get the chance.

William, 15

I feel one of the most important functions of education is to teach one to speak, to be articulate, to hold an intelligent conversation. Sure, it's fine to have a list of academic qualifications – but far better if one has the power to express views, ideas and be articulate. What use are qualifications if one can't communicate with others? Suddenly in the sixth forms one is expected to talk and debate – but this must be part of the coaching from the beginning. Far better to replace constipated ways of teaching with more active lessons, with teachers and pupils discussing, for oral lessons would constitute a livelier, more vital atmosphere.

M. (boy), 17

A school where the teacher is regarded as a friend and yet
  respected;
Where the barrier of the desk is overcome,
And learning is a series of discussions and experiments;
Where the formidable word 'lesson' is incomprehensible,
For there are no lessons as such,
And yet we learn more willingly than before.

Susy, 17

Lessons should be interesting and not a drag (like the boring English teacher who repeated the same paragraph from 'Classical Stories' about nine times before remembering about the time 'he was a little boy', which is also equally uninteresting), and more

63

varied than 'Shakespeare' and 'Chaucer', although at times they can be interesting or tragic as the case may be.

Carol, 16

I always think it is most important for a subject to be taught *interestingly*, and not for it to be hurried or driven at all the time. The worst thing in a lesson is boredom. If one is bored, you just lose interest and don't attend or learn. If one is interested, one can pick up facts and remember them for a long time afterwards. I think a common mistake is for teachers to say, 'I am going to tell you this and I want you to listen carefully and remember all the details about which you shall have a test afterwards. . . .' Then when the story or speech or lecture comes along you are worried about remembering and listening. When a person's mind is not at rest, how can you remember? It is much better for a teacher *not* to mention a test, but tell the story (or speech or lecture) interestingly, then test you afterwards. I think people are much more likely to remember facts if they *enjoy* having them told. A story helps, or plenty of adjectives.

Janet, 13

. . . the basic premise is that the teacher and the school have unlimited faith in the capabilities of the pupil. The children must exist in an atmosphere where they can fully and entirely respond to the people and objects around them. A child who is blandly presented with a difficult English text to précis, or who has to copy a mass of fact concerning fossils covering a blackboard, will in the majority of cases react unfavourably. How much better it would be to let this child write a vivid description of some deep and moving experience, or to go out and discover for himself some interesting rock or fossil.

Kenneth, 17

Sometimes, the idea of learning about people who lived before us, or in other parts of the world, interests me, and yet, when I go to a geography lesson: 'Name three rivers in France.' 'Where is copper found in Africa?' Plastic relief maps would help me considerably to visualize a country; the difficulties in this one, the route to that port. If we were given this type of map of Brazil, say, with little buildings made of plastic, on a rubber base, and little suckers on the underside, to stick on to the map; fields of the same substance with the name printed across; arrows symbolizing winds to lay on; ships, animals, roads; all this would add interest to the lessons.

Nina, 14

Lessons must be a mixture or combined effort by teacher, machine and pupil. Often a teacher will come out with something amusing, and this livens up a dull lesson a lot. Also the unexpected throwing away of routine in a school helps to make it less of the prison it appears to be for some.

Nina, 14

My scheme would need many more teachers than the present one, but this would be possible, I hope, because teaching would become a more attractive profession. The emphasis would shift from feeding with facts to developing the individual mind. It would be impossible any longer to think of a pupil as an 'A' or 'D' stream type because everyone would be recognized as a personality with good qualities to cherish. Although no teacher would churn out the same notes year after year, he would find his job more stimulating and would also have opportunities for his own research.

Rachel, 17

History to many is just pages of dates. This should not be so. History is also fossil hunts and visits to museums and castles.

R. (boy), 11

History can be the most fascinating and also the most boring of all school 'subjects'. Four years ago, in the primary school, we crouched spellbound as the snake's prey before the glittering eyes of the Roman gladiator who clashed, smeared in dust, sweat and blackened blood, round the arena. One year later, tall flashing knights knelt in proud obeisance to queens with grave eyes and jewelled robes. The threadbare, red-and-white banners crumpled in salute – to ourselves. Then, a scrunch of pebbles, a sucking of wavelets, a fanfare of golden trumpets, and grim William stood, shedding an aura of power and determination on Hastings' sandy dunes. A red swirl of events followed, until Drake's towering, creamy sails billowed to the firmament before a wild wind. But the sails fluttered and died, and the wind skirled over the edge of the world into black nothingness. It has never come back.

At the end of the third year I drew a line under 'History' in a printed form. I have since been labouring my way through a grey, mechanical tangle of drudgery, or 'British Social and Economic History, 1700 ———'. Actually, I enjoyed, relatively speaking, the two separate weeks on agriculture, as some groping feeler for the lost, pulsing freshness of life. The remaining fourth-year history (four periods a week, on, on, on) was engulfed under a jarring flood of facts, machines, names and dates. I now know by heart a long list of inventions in the eighteenth-century textile industry: John Kay, Flying Shuttle, 1733 ... spinning machine with rollers, 1738 – it didn't work anyway; just how many tons of coal were produced at the most unlikely dates throughout the two centuries, the physical mechanisms of Watt's steam engine, Bramah's patent water-closet and Nasmyth's steam hammer, as well as a host of other fragments. Shattered and flung about like the splinters of a broken jam-jar, how can all this superficial knowledge be gathered into the swelling, fluctuating flow of life which must have been there?

If I could reform my school I should do it on the principle of education through each pupil's own imagination.... It seems to me that it is the bored, fidgety pupils who cause the hold-ups (I speak from the same level). If everyone is kept intelligently amused, eagerness to carry on discovering history will surely follow. Interest should be maintained through films, group projects and discussions, not lectures. Pupils should be exhorted to imagine, imagine themselves there in the dirty mills or lofty House of Lords, imagine people talking, making decisions through lengthy arguments or sudden whims. Questions: 'What sort of *man* was Napoleon?' 'Do you think personal character had any influence on these political decisions?' should be posed, sometimes for class discussion, sometimes for homework, which could include projects and research with a few essays. . . .

I awake to a sickening thud each Monday morning – double History, eighty minutes of the toneless drone of the master's voice and the pendulum swing of his leg over the desk.

Judith, 14

I would like
to stand on the Seventh Hill at sunset,
seeing in my mind's eye seven birds,
their black shapes cleaving the soft billows of cloud
as they fly across the wrinkled Cloth-of-Gold into the sun.

I would like
to stand at midday
in the centre of an amphitheatre,
seeing in my mind's eye the savage sweating crowd
emitting a low menacing murmur
for the slaughter to begin.

I would like
to visit a ruined temple on a hill,
with seagulls wheeling about the crumbling pillars:
to kneel at dusk before the broken altar,
the heavy smell of incense in my nostrils,
wondering if their gods still haunt the empty tabernacles.

I would like
to wander down the Appian Way, and commune with their spirits:
lame Claudius who was too high-minded,

Brutus, torn between two loyalties,
Caesar, his bitter glory still lingering on
(his blood is on our hands),
and all the men who loved Rome,
with her glory, pride, debauchery and gradual decay,
who committed murder and betrayed their brothers
in her name.

They say that Rome has not died, she only sleeps –
yet through all my pages of Latin verbs
I have not felt her stir.

Gillian, 15

The English lesson could be so interesting if only it were allowed to be. Instead of a book of *Macbeth*, why don't we go to see *Macbeth*, and then discuss it afterwards; perhaps even act it afterwards, but let us recognize and understand the plot before we start.

Lynne, 15

If in English you were describing running, fighting, standing on your head, or anything active you have feelings about, you would leave the classroom and do the action in question.

Ruth, 13

English in many schools (including our own) consists of notes, notes, notes on poets and authors, etc. Why they wrote that book or poem, what they are trying to tell you in writing it. Lessons on clauses and phrases, etc., are not that important. Surely it is more important to get us to write our own poems and plays. We should be encouraged to write freely about things. Drama is important because as well as writing freely we ought to be able to express ourselves freely.

Ruth, 15

P S. **If they taught English** this letter would be in better condition than what it is.

Carol, 16

From a letter from an imaginary head of the English department in a comprehensive school, describing an ideal method of English teaching.

... we are obliged to teach in a way that is acceptable to children of varying degrees of intelligence and from different backgrounds. We make no attempt to stream the children until the end of the third year, when we begin to think about what exams they should take. A new exam system reduces the risk of failing or passing because of an uncharacteristic performance on a single day, and ensures that the children work throughout the year. Half the marks are allocated to test essays, set and marked by the school staff, with the approval of the examining board. The children are taught in groups of twelve until they reach the sixth form. They then attend lectures, which are complemented by seminars, where questions are raised and essays set and marked. This, I hope, serves as a brief description of the framework within which we teach.

The English department aims to teach the children how effectively to communicate with one another, and how to enjoy and understand literature, thus helping them to develop into adults who understand themselves and can give valuable service to others. We try to carry the children's interest outside the classroom by running various societies for drama, poetry and creative writing. We find the latter acts as an invaluable emotional safety valve, as well as helping them to appreciate the difficulties of other authors and giving them first-hand experience of the beauty and intractability of language.

'Language,' writes Wesker, 'is words. It's bridges so that you can get safely from one place to another. And the more bridges you know about, the more places you can see.' We do not want any of our children to suffer from limitations that unfamiliarity with their own language and its uses may impose on them. We study language at work in society and in literature, and do very few exercises, as these are not really helpful in understanding the nature and functions of language. The children write advertisements, newspaper reports, political speeches, and official documents, sometimes deliberately imitating the style of the original, sometimes creating a novel style of their own. We introduce them to their own peculiar language, to local dialect, and trace it to its origins. We then connect it with the history of the language as a whole. By this time, they are beginning to regard language as a fascinating subject in its own right, rather than simply as a passport to every other subject.

In the teaching of literature, we aim to educate the appreciative and critical sense in the children in such a way that it becomes, not only active but well-informed. We hope that they will then always be able to derive pleasure and profit from literature and discern its value. We try to confine ourselves to works which deal with events and feelings with which the children are familiar at first, and allow them a certain amount of choice in what they read, in the hope that we will not cause them to shy away from literature by making them read books which they are too young to appreciate. The children are taught speech and drama as part of their English course, and we try to impress on them the essential difference between the written and spoken word. We never simply read plays. We act them out on an improvised stage in a motley collection of costumes. We never read poetry to ourselves, but always aloud. Real, live poets come to talk to the children. Desk-bound discussions of the text follow only when it has been properly introduced as a work of art.

We, the staff, all have a sincere belief in the importance of what we are doing, and we can only hope that the children will profit from and remember their lessons, for as Golding writes: 'The arts cannot cure a disease or increase production or ensure defence. They can only cure or ameliorate sicknesses so deeply seated that we begin to think of them as built-in boredom and satiety, selfishness and fear.'

Janet, 18

From two visions of the future.
English next class – I hope we carry on planning our film. I'm art director and heroine – my life is so busy – I love every minute.

We're aching to start timing our shooting script, but Stephen felt he had to give us a little discussion on our coming G.C.U.s (General Certificate of Understanding). He told us how the examiners of each subject will be previously informed of all we have done during the past years and during the 'exam' will discuss with each one of us different aspects of our work. . . .

Linda, 15

In a light, airy room I find Chris, the lecturer, already seated, surrounded by a semi-circle of thirteen boys and girls comfortably clad in civilian clothes. Chris tells us of research into the life of King George III, throwing light on the latter's mysterious 'fits of insanity'. An animated political argument over the effect George III's ideas would have on the British public of today follows, then we disperse into the library to read about the policies of Pitt the Younger and to record our findings in our folders.

At 2.30 we have mathematics taught by Alan, an enthusiastic young man, new out of university, whose speciality is logic. He delights in setting us complicated problems about A, B and C, which we solve by discovering which owns what and lives where, etc. He also deals with graphs concerning social statistics – this afternoon, the rise in the number of illegitimate children born each year. Alan suggests I read about architecture, because it may arouse my artistic side as well as encouraging my mathematics.

Four o'clock means the end of another ninety-minute lesson and a short break. French begins at a quarter past the hour. Today Hélène decides to interest us in French authors instead of continuing the routine 'cabin' work. She instructs us to choose a writer, considering both his/her works and private life, and my pick is the controversial Colette. Towards the end of the lesson, Hélène interrupts our reading to ask our opinion of some poems by Jacques Prévert.

We finish our day at 5.45 and sign ourselves out at the secretary's office. Unless we ourselves wish to follow up some topic, the evening is our own. I walk along the road in a daze, my dream fading, slowly coming back to reality and my grim, Gothic-fronted grammar school.

Nicola, 16

Mathematics is always a tricky subject. Some find it easy – because they are very good at mental arithmetic, but run into difficulties when reasoning power is needed; other can see the reasoning, know the method but fall down on the arithmetic; and some are just confused. Those types must all be taught differently.

Nina, 14

Mathematics is no longer connected with the time it takes a train at 117½ m.p.h. to travel from London to Glasgow via Hull. Nor is it anything to do with how much water enters a bath in seven minutes if tap A is full on, tap B half on and the plughole open. Yet we are still taught how to calculate the answers to these and other trivial problems. The answers could be obtained quicker, easier and more correctly by the use of a desk-calculator. With the invention of micro-electronics, and the subsequent development of cheaper, more compact computers, it is hard to see why any of the present arithmetical mathematics should be taught at all. At my perfect school, computer-programming would be taught as a separate subject, while mathematics would be concerned with mathematical theories, such as group theory, set theory, non-Euclidean geometries and number theory. These are considered by some experts to be some of the most powerful tools of modern mathematics.

Alan, 16

New maths doesn't make any sense – just all measuring things that one will hardly ever have to measure in real life.

Isabel, 11

I usually enjoy maths lessons, but there is one which sticks in my mind as one I hated. We had been learning about various aspects of map-making and suddenly our maths master said that we were to split into small groups and make a map of the school and grounds. After giving a few words of explanation, he produced some measuring equipment and there was a mad scramble for it. When that rush was over, there was another rush – this time for the door. All of this was accompanied by loud chatter which must have disturbed the whole school. Outside there was a lot of larking about, plus, of course, noise, and complaints were received from all parts of the school. We were given a week to produce our maps, and at the end of the week only one was finished. That week's maths lessons were the worst I can remember, and I was thoroughly fed up as were several other boys by the end of the week.

Jeremy, 15

The school I'd like would be, like me, old-fashioned – but not too old-fashioned. It would *not* have about six projects a term – only about one. The reason for this is that I get very tired of having to bring newspaper cuttings, matchboxes, etc., to school every day, and knowing that by the time we have finished one project, there's always another looming up.

Isabel, 11

Not all lessons can be helped by practical methods of teaching. You can't really ask the staff to recreate the Battle of Austerlitz on the cricket pitch. Classrooms will stay because they do have their uses.

Jennifer, 15

Our schools have become unfriendly, boring slums; our 'teachers' uninterested adults fighting a losing battle. . . . This cannot be the fault of the pupils. Even though the older generation frequently attacks the youth of today as being 'untidy, rude and lazy', it seems evident from such philosophies as that of the flower children that the younger generation is attempting to formulate

73

its own ideas. It is the conditions in schools today that help greatly to create the impression that we are 'untidy, rude and lazy.' Nobody can be greatly inspired (and this is speaking from personal experience) by ... the boring, antique, blackboard-and-book methods.

By teaching with books – textbooks being the heart and soul of teaching today – no practical experience of any subject is gained. Everything learnt is second hand if it comes from the teachers, and very often out of date and misleading if it comes from the books – these could just as easily be read at home, with greater concentration and better results. I would suggest discarding bookteaching and, with the money saved, running practical courses. ... Of course books cannot be forgotten. Indeed, the reading of books should be encouraged; but it must be private reading, done at home, whilst the day at school will magnify practically what we have read. The reading will be in place of homework – that archaic system whereby a lot of important work is rushed through or just ignored. After all, why should we continue our studies when school has finished for the day? In the evening we, the schoolchildren, want to enjoy ourselves or just relax, and if a lot of homework stands in our way then we will leave it until later, which means late nights and a bad morning to follow, to spoil it by hurrying. A book will provide the relaxation for many, but no matter how the time is spent, relaxation is essential.

Richard, 17

If they must give us homework, let's have another hour at school, that's where our rulers and pens are, as well as the rest of our tools.

K. (boy), 14

Homework should *not* be given. Many of us would rather spend another hour at school than two hours at home doing 'an hour's homework', where we are constantly being distracted by television and such things.

Irena, 15

The usual concept of a school is one of a place where young people are assembled to learn facts. This is the major thing I would change. What is the point of taking facts from a book and teaching them to pupils? In a book, facts are in logical order and correct; while in the brain of the average pupil they are muddled and frequently wrong. Surely it is far better to leave the facts in convenient books and to teach the pupils to think. Obviously, certain facts and abilities (such as reading) will have to be taught, but the fewer the better. These would be taught at the equivalent of the present infant schools.

Alan, 17

The people who write textbooks do not make mistakes – and the best way to learn is by your own mistakes.

Jennifer, 15

More free periods should be given so that notes taken during a film could be developed into an interesting essay. The essays could be kept together and at the end of the syllabus a book could be compiled which would be nearly as good as the convenient textbook but twice as interesting.

D. (boy), 15

Scientific principles and theories can be more clearly explained and understood using films, as it is easier to believe what we see with our own eyes than what a book or a teacher assures us is true.

Angela, 15

A lesson is not much good if, for instance in science, all one ever does is listen to the teacher instead of finding out things for ourselves. After all, why have fifteen bunsen burners if the only person who ever uses one is the master?

R. (boy), 11

As a student of German and Russian, I can only speak on behalf of the arts side. All my grammar and syntax has been learnt from

75

time-worn, smelly little books.... So far, only first-year French is taught by a modern method – the audio-visual system, the only components of which appear to be a decrepit projector and massive exercise books. This, so far as I can see, does not go far enough.

Peter, 17

... **by the end of the fifth year** we are perfectly capable of sitting down and translating a page of English into French, but would be completely tongue-tied if asked to hold a short conversation with a French person.

Beverley, 15

A French baby learns to talk first and then write; in my school this should be how it is done.

Paul, 15

One thing I would like to see would be teaching as impartial as possible. Many children are taught ideas not their own, and are not encouraged to develop ideas of their own. This is where, I think, the teaching machine comes into its own. It deals in plain facts, and leaves the pupil to interpret them as he or she may wish. It also does not make mistakes, and if it breaks down it can easily be put right. Most teachers say that machines could never replace a human being, as if that was the sole purpose of them. But teaching aids such as these are not and never will be able to do this, and this is not what they were meant for. All a teaching aid can do is to aid the teacher – nothing more.

George, 14

Today's media – television, films, radio – should be used in lessons. How many students have been told 'Write an appreciation of last night's *Wednesday Play*'. 'Do you think Paul Scofield deserved an Oscar for his part in *A Man for all Seasons*?'

Paul, 15

Teaching itself
brought nearer to the natural lines that are
followed instinctively by parents with their offspring
(adapted, focused, to the special course
of language, mathematics, history).
For education, simply, is a facet
of childhood preparation for the lives
children are born to lead;
it must walk hand in hand
with what they learn within their families.

W. (boy), 17

All Kids Are Equal

The children who do worst under our system – the slow, the backward, the retarded – were, naturally enough, least well represented among these essayists. Some have stated their case, often by implication, elsewhere in this book. However, a few children with other backgrounds spoke for them very directly, and a handful of such statements I have collected in this section, together with a wry blast from a sufferer, and a final pronouncement by a child who was the only one to point to one of the most obvious inequities in our system : that your educational fate depends to a sometimes quite freakish extent on your address.

The building would be spacious with only the minimum of pupils, so that each pupil would have a little more individual attention. Not as in the schools of my environment, where the children with less ability than others are just pushed aside (this is true of schools all over the country) and given no attention, and given the name of Cs and Ds. Where the teachers can merrily leave them until it is time to leave school, when these poor people will be left to the mercy of the world. Because these are the people who will be most easily swindled. In my mind, the children should be given equal rights, because surely the children with a higher standard of intelligence are in need of less help than those with a low standard. I am not saying that the children with a higher standard of intelligence should be abandoned, but equal attention should be given to all. The ones with a lower grade of intelligence would have teachers specially assigned to try and bring their sleeping talents out into the open air.

Lynn, 14

There should be none thought of as an 'average pupil'. We should be allowed to set our own speed. In this way the slow ones could keep up and the ones who can work quickly need not spend half the lesson being bored.

Irena, 15

The school to which I was sent at age eleven was a secondary modern school. A new headmaster was in charge of this bricked building, which had tight steel window-frames and a wind-proof corridor by the playground that let in the rain because it was bounded by a low wall and no windows.

The main hall windows saw the pupils eating their shilling's-worth of school dinner each (there was no proper dining hall); these dinners were cooked in a 'temporary' 1939 cookhouse that was as old as the school. However, at eleven years of age such a wonderful place as this was fairly tolerable. I was made tolerant (they estimated our eleven-plus results from last year's work) with several others from class two of the junior school, while the class one dunces were posted to Worthlewise Grammar.

Nevertheless all kids are equal, and as far as I knew we all were equal here, and our parents had been told it was a good school, and where to buy our caps and blazers.

Most of our fathers – staff – were good blokes. Some of them had attended technical schools, and after these were abolished people thought in terms of 'secondary grammar' or 'secondary modern' schools; but now 'secondary' as applied to a grammar school has disappeared and been forgotten. They just think 'Secondary or grammar'. That word 'secondary' infers so much.

These good blokes were not as well academically qualified as they could be, but they did not need high qualifications to teach the worst-behaved, scruffiest load of idiots who were branded with the good name of the school to start with.

The lessons were very informative. The amount of homework set in our first year was not much greater in quantity than that actually set in our sixth. The homework contained useless, convergent exercises, and we had some help from teacher over the spelling mistakes. Although told by our parents, when young, that we 'must go to school to learn', most of us here were not learned to spell !

For me, there is still a little magic left in that building with the wind-proof corridor. For the many who left at fifteen, whether good enough for the G.C.E. or not, there is none. A great pity indeed. For at present no schoolboy of fifteen in Great Britain is eligible for a student grant.

Here I have shown, I hope, the not untrue meaning of secondary school life today. Such schools as the one I have described above – the show schools of pre-war years – should be rebuilt to realistic criteria.

J. (boy), 17

The ideal school for the present day would be entirely comprehensive – infant, junior and secondary education being completed under one roof – but making provision for change if desired. It would be advantageous in several ways. One: making a more even distribution of staff to schools, which in turn would standardize the size of classes to a large extent, relieving overcrowding in some areas. Two: one of the worst faults of contemporary education would be cut out – the practice of having a sharp break in schooling at the age of eleven; a bad practice because, first, it makes no allowance for individual rates of development – as a consequence of which many children are sent to the wrong type of school for their capabilities; second, there can be an emotional effect on sensitive children which will adversely affect their work. A third advantage would be that the behaviour and characteristics of each child could be studied, making it easier for the head teacher to give a reference at the end of his school life and contributing to the child's welfare by greater understanding of his personality.

Jennifer, 18

Because I think that the eleven-plus is very unfair and I am all for everyone having the same chances of education, streaming would be necessary. But it should be arranged in such a way that each child would be in good streams for good subjects and bad streams for bad subjects, and not in a bad stream for every subject if they were not very academic.

Caroline, 14

Another stupidity that I have come across during my school life is the level of difficulty between two eleven-plus papers – one for the York district, including the East and West Ridings, the other for the North Riding. No slightly above-ordinarily intelligent child can get through the North Riding exam. They have to be practically superhuman to pass it. But if the parents want the child to have a good education they have to pay for it. I avoided the North Riding exam by only a hundred yards. What is the difference where a child lives? He will probably move away to some other town or district before he is twenty-one to find a better job. But just because he happened to live on a piece of land called the North Riding he has less chance of going to grammar school. It should not matter whether he lives on one of the islands north of Scotland or at Land's End; he should have exactly the same chance of going to a grammar school. Who knows what clever people in England could have benefited her greatly but for a useless, senseless boundary-line that said they were not good enough?

Valerie, 16

Lessons Ought to Mix

It is a curious experience, for anyone who has been attentive to educational thinking in recent years, to read what these children say about the curriculum. It has been widely agreed that the barriers between subjects are too rigid. There has been much talk of breaking them down. It seemed reasonable to assume that in a sample of 1,000 schoolchildren, some at least would have had experience of a curriculum that had lost some of its subject-bound character. And yet there is little if any sign of this in these essays, and the children's most common plea is (in the forthright words of one of them) '*Lessons ought to mix.*'

Great hatred of subject barriers simply as devices that break up the school day into a series of small dissociated experiences! Detestation of bells which ring just as you may have become interested in what you are doing! What effect can all that talk about integrating subjects have had, when so many children still suffer from conventional timetables in which thirty or forty minutes of maths is followed by thirty or forty minutes of history, and then by leaps or lurches into equally brief and detached bouts of English, geography, French and all the rest?

If anyone doubted that the subject boundaries ought to be blurred, or that the daily timetable ought at least to have more coherence than it commonly has, these children must surely convince them of the case. For the fact is that most of them fairly writhe under the typical organization of school work. They do so not only because it makes the day such a frustrating patchwork, but also because they feel the need to over-ride those old barriers. Life is not like this, they seem to be saying, it is not a series of unconnected compartments. A human being doesn't think wholly separate historical thoughts, geographical thoughts, English thoughts. At the same time, life (when conditions are reasonable) doesn't limit human activity in any field to mere half-hours. The trouble, when things are chopped up like this, is that you can't anywhere put down real roots. And the children want to put down roots, deep into human learning.

So they call for new kinds of curriculum, in which they can follow up a wave of interest until it is, for the moment, spent; or in which a number of associated subjects are made to serve a single inquiry (they suggest various ways this might be done). They want projects, and to be allowed to build their work out of all sorts of subject matter round central interests. They want a new flexibility of routine out of which might come learning as a coherent experience.

And behind such demands lies the almost scornfully convinced sense many of them have that the old content of education is quite inadequate to our times. Again and again they ask to be introduced to philosophy, psychology, logic; to learn about current affairs, politics, modern machines, human relationships, local government, budgeting. You would think, says a boy, that such highly important human concerns (he happened to be thinking specially of the Highway Code and the workings of a motorcar engine) were 'almost leprous', so carefully are they avoided by most schools. It is not, as I read it, the gleam of novelty the children are after. They are certainly ambitious, and of course there is an element in their demands of the desire to be doing work that has some grandeur about it. This need of the young to be grand, as students, is a quality in them that I believe we waste, outrageously. But what they seem really to be groping for is some system of learning, some arrangement of the curriculum, that gathers together the old subjects, and adds more, and creates out of it all some meaningful total experience. That is surely the point of these constant references to larger, compound disciplines, to philosophy and psychology and logic and the study of political structures, which are all capable of drawing on knowledge gained in various fields to provide general views of the human enterprise. Heavens, yes, that is what the children are after : big views, a gathering together of things learnt.

It is for just such reasons that many of them also want 'unusual languages', or studies that bridge the gulf between the sciences and the arts – or simply much more art, or a wider choice of recreation. It is why they want girls to invade the boys' territory, and vice versa; why, again, some of them would like the school to be a base, to which an old pupil might return with his problems. As things are, the school curriculum, and the timetable that accomodates it, serves all those ends that, throughout these essays, the children have rejected – the ends of segregation and disunity, so that subject can be divorced from subject, the teacher can play a role that keeps him aloof from his pupil, leisure and labour can be sharply distinguished, boys can be boys and girls can be girls, and school itself can provide an experience detached from the rest of life. This won't do any longer, they say, this compartmented learning, which offers no big views, at the same time as it excludes quite specific pieces of learning that children sensibly see they require about income tax and family allowances and 'how to live continuously with another human being'. A great many of our 1,000 children, at any rate, see in a wholly new curriculum, at once much more coherent and more flexible than the common present arrangement, a means of giving to their schooling the excitement of unity and of a sense of general purpose and direction.

Ideally the school would have a wide curriculum, students would not be walled-in by subject discipline, confined by maths, physics and chemistry, but would study more subjects, seeing these in the light of the plethora of knowledge surrounding them, thus learning a toleration and appreciation of studies with which they are not immediately concerned.

Ann, 18

I think lessons ought to mix, not keep strictly to themselves as they do in most secondary schools. In the school I'd like there would be no lessons as such, but you would be given a syllabus for each subject at the beginning of each year. If you wanted information about something you would go to the filing room in the block which deals with that particular subject. In the filing room all the information needed would be stored in alphabetical order. If you cannot find it or you need help you go to the teacher in his (or her) room.

Judith, 12

Today's school day is chopped into strictly regimented sections broken up by the jarring ring of the electric bell. The school rumbles into action from one lesson to the next, wasting ten minutes in between. Thus, just as a subject has become absorbing and interesting it is locked away until the next lesson and the mind is switched to a new wavelength for the next subject. This continual interruption makes the work become boring and the pupil loses interest. In tomorrow's school the work will be continued until it is finished or a suitable pause has been reached.

Janet, 16

I feel that the timetable should be linked together in such a way that the lessons link up with each other and the mind can continue in the same frame of thinking, instead of being broken up by a bell.

Danny, 15

I like changing from one lesson to another although they may not be connected in any way. I think this keeps the mind alert.

Elizabeth, 15

I believe the first step necessary is to dilute, or even destroy, rigid arbitrary divisions chopping up schooling into nicely compact subjects. This division is by its very nature an artificial imposition that can only impede and misrepresent the natural flow of learning. Obviously, as the pupil attains higher levels of education, division and specialization are essential, but prior to this in primary and the lower age groups of secondary schools, the various subjects should be, and should be seen to be, closely allied and inter-related. This integration of subjects should be based primarily on the vast amount of experience potentially available from outside the rather restrictive walls of school. For example, a focal point can be decided upon, say an interesting old church, and from this central point can spring associated studies, such as its historical development, the geographical reasons for its location, the mathematical principles involved in its construction, the form of religion going on inside it, and so on. Additionally its imagery and emotional impact can be re-created in the pupil's mind by paints, sculpture, words and possibly music. It is evident that something in this nature would necessitate the complete co-operation of the subjects involved and would certainly be far less convenient than more traditional methods, but I feel that it is more important that the gulfs between subjects should be diminished.

Kenneth, 17

A deadening influence in school is routine. Instead of obeying a set timetable, I would prefer to have my weekly quota of lessons supplied and go to them in whichever order I liked, according to mood. Thus a drifting atmosphere would replace rigid routine.

Elizabeth, 16

The function of a school is presumably to teach its pupils how to enjoy and how to make the best use of the world in which we live. In fact, nearly all the subjects which are taught in schools, however purely 'academic' they may seem, are fundamentally related to man or to his environment, but the relationship is often not obvious. Because what does exist, or has existed, is taught in our schools under the superficial names of 'Geography' or 'History', very little attention is paid to what might exist, and so the benefit of the acquired knowledge is never properly used. For this reason, the first requirement of the teachers in my ideal school would be that they be interesting as people, and capable of transforming dry knowledge into the art of living.

... the main aim of my school would be that the pupils learn how to make best use of (that is, to understand) the world through effective knowledge. This would involve the breakdown of conventional subject disciplines. The new divisions would be more comprehensive; for instance, since more people are interested in themselves and other people, the study of 'Human Lives and

Living' would play a large part in the curriculum. It would include psychology, human biology, geography, history and philosophy, besides aspects of human living represented in art such as family relationships in classical Greek drama. As regards the last aspect, drama, the question which the schoolchildren would be patiently but persistently asked to consider would be, 'How should I react in a similar situation?' Intimate discussion between small groups of pupils would be encouraged, it goes without saying, so that the fruits of individual work and thought could be collected and united by the children themselves. This method would teach the pupils that outside school life the class–teacher relationship is, fortunately, not a common one.

Elizabeth, 17

Each subject would be allotted one day per week or more, depending on the number of subjects chosen for study. A very large syllabus would be set each term, thus making it unlikely that anyone would finish it.

Lorraine, 15

I would go around asking the pupils what they would like to be when they grow up and whatever someone has in mind, e.g. a nurse, I would let her work in the laboratories and I would ask the science teacher to help her with her work as much as possible. If a pupil likes a certain sport such as tennis I would ask the P.E. teacher to coach him or her as much as possible and forget useless games like rounders.

Angela, 13

There should be extensive departments for every possible subject range, and the choices and combinations of subjects should be entirely unrestricted. For example, no pupils would be flatly informed that he or she must study one of the following: music, history or geography. I am quoting this case from my experience. Marvellous it may have been for those few brilliantly gifted musicians, or for those natural historians, or for those to whom geographical features come as easily as breathing. However, geography, music, history and chemistry and physics just are not my gifted subjects. I have very little or no interest in any of them, and about as much ability. The only way high marks can be gained in these unwanted subjects is to learn parrot-fashion all the facts and notes dictated by the member of staff concerned. In my opinion this is pointless and is the worst way of educating any intelligent human being. The subject should be studied, explored, practised and experiments should be carried out. It should not be learnt just to be recited; it must be understood. If we were not obliged, or rather compelled, to take the subjects which we have no inclination for, we could use the valuable time to supplement that spent on more favourable topics. For this reason I think that, if desired by the individual, he should spend all his time on his chosen subjects and not waste it on those which hold no interest for him. Then fewer subjects could be worked on in greater detail and to a more advanced depth. Of course, the pupil has the choice : either to take several subjects generally, or to specialize in one or two.

Patricia, 15

Granted, our present system allows for a certain amount of freedom in learning with its slogan : let them experiment to find a conclusion rather than provide the conclusion, telling them to prove it.

However, this freedom, although made use of at primary level, is rarely bestowed upon secondary school pupils – except perhaps in their sixth and final year – who are forced to adhere rigidly to a set timetable. Could not this educational liberty be moved from the youngest to the oldest pupils? Could not all the 'necessary' time-table work be done at primary level, leaving the older pupil, grounded in the basis of each subject, to further his knowledge at his own speed, exploiting his freedom to the full? Surely much more knowledge would be gathered this way by willing pupils than at present, when someone who prefers modern poetry must first read Keats, and one thirsting for knowledge of the ancients is bombarded with the policies of Lloyd George?

Janet, 15

When boys came to the school they would be asked what they were particularly interested in. If about a dozen boys said they were particularly interested in architecture then they would be able to build something. At first they would only be allowed to build a less important building like a shed for the pitch roller. This would include plenty of the separate subjects in an interesting and exciting way. When planning the building, maths and technical drawing would be learnt. The making of the materials would include woodwork. The actual building would include geography and a certain amount of physical exercise. Then at the end the boys would each be expected to write a separate report on what they had done. This would cover English. Later the boys could do bigger jobs and also study the history of building.

Stephen, 13

The object is to promote creative ability in the individual, and not simply to present facts. In the future the school will try to present material so that the student will become deeply involved and interested in his work; for the student who enjoys his work is always the one who makes good progress and understands his work as opposed to simply learning it. To this end there would be no such things as set 'lessons' and boundaries between subjects would be freely crossed.

Now, the development of creativity is a difficult task and cannot be taught in the conventional sense. A mind cannot be made to produce creative thoughts; it can only be shown, and given practice in the conditions which are likely to produce creativity ...

K. (boy), 17

Attending school would not be compulsory, but for the first term curiosity, parents and habit would bring the newcomers with regularity to school every morning. Those developing an interest in a certain subject, at any age, would surely attend school to go to these lessons. . . . Those pupils who at first profess not to care about such worldly things as exams would soon think again on seeing their classmates passing out of the school qualified and obtaining excellent jobs. With the free and happy atmosphere of the establishment, friendship would come easily, making attendance at school regular so that the pupils could see their friends among both the pupils and the staff.

The staff, of course, would have to be ready to be called on by worried or enthusiastic pupils at any time to teach or give help or advice at school, and perhaps even at home. They must be constantly ready to give tactful guidance to all pupils.

Vanessa, 16

... **the pupils would be divided** into forms of fifteen to twenty children by a purely arbitrary method, such as the initial of the surname. The teacher who had responsibility for the form, and might change every two years, would help each pupil to choose his own curriculum, on the basis of his interests and abilities. The pupil's 'projects' would be the cornerstone of his education; these would range from 'Find out what you can about seventeenth-century costume, make some drawings and decide what kind of life the people who wore the different types of clothes led' for the twelve-year-olds to 'Learn the rudiments of a new language' for the older pupils.

The project might last for a week or a month or a year. Practical work would not be excluded, and this seems to me a particularly good way of teaching mathematics and science. Teachers would be available to assist, if only in the early stages of the project, as would all possible books and equipment. Projects that took the pupils outside the school boundaries would be encouraged. Discussion groups would often be formed, and working in threes and fours would be perfectly permissible and especially helpful when friends had been separated by the arrangement of forms.

The teacher would have not only the responsibility of helping in the choice of studies, but also that of deciding when a pupil might have two projects concurrently, when a project had no longer any value, and when perseverance was the better course. He would also occasionally have to prise some pupils away from beloved specialist subjects.

Once a term each pupil would present his best project for

consideration, so that the head teacher could gauge his progress. Public examinations would still exist, but a pass would depend on the quality of a project chosen from a wide range of topics, and taken with the answer to a general question under normal examination conditions whose answer would depend on an ability to handle either facts or abstract ideas. For example, *Project*: The Russian Revolution of 1917. *General question*: either 'How do you explain the success of Communism? Suggest some possibilities for its immediate future,' or 'Trace Russia's part in the First World War.'

As well as being arranged in forms, the students would be arranged in groups. These would have fifty to sixty members, representative of the age spectrum, including pupils from the sixth-form college and also, perhaps, the last year of the primary school. One or two hours a week would be devoted to their activities. The groups would arrange social service efforts where regular, reliable visits to a lonely old person would be considered more praiseworthy than a vast sum raised by an inter-class beano. Much of the school's sport, drama and music would emanate from the groups, and they would be encouraged by competitions. These groups would, I hope, apart from doing something worthwhile, combat the extreme individualism and loss of unity from which my school might otherwise suffer, and they would forge connexions between the school and its neighbourhood. But the groups would not become after-school activity clubs. There would be no school scout group, no school Duke of Edinburgh Award Scheme, because I would not want my pupils' lives devoted to the school.

Rachel, 17

There are several choices for the pupil to choose from. There are extensive libraries where he may go for project and reading work, there is a science block and an arts block, covering many aspects of art, such as still life, pottery and carpentry; and, in another block, lectures and discussions are being carried on, on all subjects from birth control in India to amphibians or trigonometry.

Linda, 16

It is important that the school must not become a prison; it should be treated more or less as an H.Q. from which studies are made. In this way students would report events as they see them verbatim, attempt to interpret them and then 'instruct' the teacher. In the ensuing discussion one hopes the truth will emerge.

I feel limited overnight accomodation should be provided for maturer students. These could be used to spend a night or two away from home occasionally, especially at times of stress.

In general there would be no specialized study until eighteen (and preferably twenty) – apart from the pursuance of individual interests which will have developed. The aim should be flexibility : to train and re-train quickly. There would be no set university examining board syllabuses to follow rigidly. What is imparted and how it is taught is left to the individual schools and the staff concerned. The student would be given the opportunity to learn techniques of self-examination and criticism; and also would discuss individually his work and progress with his educator. Thus helping all the time to preserve the uniqueness of the individual.

All should learn of the mechanisms and processes of the human mind in psychology and behavioral study classes (scrutinizing themselves especially). These would lead to 'Marriage and Parenthood Guidance' classes, including child care, child psychology, birth control, pregnancy and, most important, how to live continuously with another human being. To this end the skills and knowledge of the Marriage Guidance Bureaux should become part of schools. At several stages in the socio-sexual instruction each student should compile his own morality and code of conduct.

Paul, 18

During their first week the eleven-year-old students are given tests : medical tests, intelligence tests, personality tests; tests to find out the relation between their physique and personality; tests to sort out the introverted child from the extraverted, the aggressive from the shy. A complete picture of each child is built up, and the information gained from the tests is kept for reference during the student's schooling. Students are at first grouped according to personality and not according to intelligence. The groups are gradually mixed. Result: the differing personality types learn to live and work with one another.

At this stage the young students are taught elementary philosophy, psychology and logic. Lessons are presented in simple form – the teachers make free use of parables, analogies and puzzles, and the students benefit immensely because a knowledge of these subjects provides a good basis for clear and critical thinking.

The first year is also a science-and-mathematics year. The students are, of course, now well prepared to study these subjects and their knowledge of logic and philosophy proves really valuable. In mathematics the Trachtenberg System is taught; using this method, the students can make amazingly rapid mental calculations, working almost like computers! In science, the emphasis is on the sciences of life – biology, botany, zoology, ecology.

The reason? Well, my 'ideal' school attempts to educate its students for an 'ideal' society – a society in which there is no need for armaments or heavy industry.

In the second year two foreign languages, French and German, are taught. The 'direct method' is used. The students are saturated with the languages. They speak no English, they see films in the language, read poetry, sing songs, listen to records. They become 'French' for two months, then for the next two they become 'German'. They learn to think and write in the languages and, after four months, are fluent in both.

The third year is given over to the study of literature, art and music, but languages are still studied. The art lessons are, I suppose, a little unconventional. Drugs are used – LSD and mescalin. Children paint after having taken drugs which heighten visual perception. Records are played to inspire the students – they make paintings of images suggested by jazz and classical music.

In the final two years all subjects are related to each other. 'Bridges' are built between art and science. For instance, the students are asked to look at a tree as objectively as possible and then make sketches and notes. They attempt to express on paper, as truthfully as possible, all their visual impressions. They are then asked to look at the same trees with an artist's eye – subjectively. Again they make sketches and paintings. When they compare their subjective sketches with their objective ones, they will begin to understand a little more about themselves.

Finally, the uses of language and propaganda are taught. The students see how the same techniques are used to sell a soap detergent, a religion or a politician. They see that men like Adolf Hitler got to power not by using rational, well-balanced arguments, but by preaching insane dogmas in a manner which appealed to the 'masses'.

At the end of their course the students emerge as creative, original, intelligent individuals.

Anthony, 18

Give me the school where, as from the age of 13–14+, we will have the chance to learn and discuss elementary *philosophy, psychology, logic, contemporary world affairs, economics, arts.* In my scale of priorities, I'll place history last. Yes, biassed history written by each nation his own way! Anyway, who cares today about the misdeeds or folly of monarchs like Charles the First, of tyrants like Cromwell, Henry Bluebeard?

Cosette, 17

Why does most modern history stop at 1939 instead of going on to 1964 or 1965 when it really is modern? Why does English concentrate on Shakespeare and Sassoon instead of Beckett and Miller, who are, let's face it, more of our age than the former? Or why does geography concentrate on 'the British Empire and our eastern colonies' instead of the Common Market and the Eastern Bloc?

Philip, 16

... **I think more thought should be given** to present-day happenings. At my school we spend eighty per cent of our history lessons on ancient history. I think learning about the last wars, etc., is more important than learning about what happened centuries ago. We should reserve some of our history lessons for present-day politics and happenings in the world.

Jane, 15

At the moment, little emphasis is put on current affairs, especially in the academic streams. (There is no O-level in it!) This is surely a vitally important subject and would also include modern history.

Jeanette, 14

Teaching would be imaginative and stimulating (no machines); many short courses would be run on the sort of subjects that the rather restrictive exam syllabuses of today do not include, such as philosophy, Mao's cultural revolution, clothes designing, the life of Mr Wilson. These courses would run for about a term; so at eighteen a pupil would have a good smattering of knowledge about twenty-four different subjects never really mentioned in ordinary school subjects.

Caroline, 14

The system of a certain set of subjects being taught is wrong; instead of, say, a child being taught geography, history and music, why can't that child do a course on making radios or studying tropical fish if he wants to? I have always been interested in engines and how to mind them, but there is unfortunately nothing like this in school.

Robin, 16

There would be less restriction on the term 'education'. Does knowledge of the Highway Code, of the workings and maintenance of a car engine, not come under the heading of education? Judging by present standards, these and other subjects are regarded as being almost leprous.

Dermot, 17

Computers, calculating machines, typewriters, lathes, drills, food mixers, television sets and cars are all part of today's and to-morrow's world. Students should be at home with such equipment.

Paul, 15

We ought to be taught the meaning of local government and how elections work. We should be told of the difference between the different parties, and the people they represent. We should also be taught about other countries' politics and have discussions on which is the best method used to govern the countries.

Ruth, 13

The government and how it works and the different political parties should be dealt with in some detail in history. Many people either do not vote at all or they just choose a name of a candidate not knowing why they voted for him at all. Politics of the major countries and why their particular system works for them should also be discussed.

Ruth, 15

Two neglected subjects, taken at random, are the so-called social 'graces' and elementary logic. The former of the two choices may seem odd, for it is assumed by the public that it is taught by teachers, and by teachers that it is taught by parents. Unfortunately, in many cases this is not so, as is amply demonstrated by the louts and hooligans that are seen so much nowadays. I feel that if pupils were, from an early age, taught a thorough grounding in good manners, tact and politeness, the world in general and teenagers in particular would be the better for it. Ideally, a person attending secondary school a vulgar, rude person would emerge, at sixteen or seventeen, an example of impeccable politeness, tact, modesty and good taste....

In the school I'd like, logic would be taught. I can already hear the cry, 'It is too hard! Do not expect secondary school children to understand logic!' My reply is that primary school children

97

can understand it. I know one boy who while still at primary school read logic to pass the time!

George, 14

In universities, psychology is a popular subject, yet while subjects such as music and physical education are taught with enthusiasm, this is never broached. I would like to know more about my fellow men and understand myself. There is so much soul-searching in the later teens that it would be of value for teachers to help one to help oneself.

Anne, 17

History and geography are dealt with adequately, but psychology and politics, drug-taking and smoking and love and death are not mentioned in the school syllabus at all.

Kari, 13

Give us a more varied syllabus! Give us the chance to visit more frequently factories, to talk with miners, dustbin men, doctors, lawyers, jail-birds and addicts too. Give us the chance to visit remand homes. Prisons like Holloway, Pentonville, Parkhurst. We want to know more about life and a bit less about books.

Cosette, 17

But what is the main purpose of schools – to educate young people so that when they go out into the world they will be prepared for it? But are they? We learn our mathematics, English, physics, etc., but what do we learn about sex, marriage and things like this? These are just as important, but we don't learn very much about them.

David, 15

Studies of child development should appear in the timetable, because the object of education is to equip the immature for maturity. As these children would have done most of their real learning by direct discovery methods, so in their senior stage they would continue this method of learning by taking responsibility for the younger children, e.g., conducting visits, helping with dinner duties, sometimes assisting during the school day.

Susan, 15, and Janet, 15

We must not let ourselves be dictated to by out-dated syllabuses. For example, tricky little questions like:

'Given that

$$q + a^2 = \left(\frac{b^2 x^3}{c^4} \right)$$

prove that u does not equal bf' are of no use to anybody. Instead contemporary problems concerning domestic economy, income-tax, rates, book-keeping and family allowances should be clarified to the students instead of useless information which is only of any purpose when doing Johnny's homework, some way off in the distant future.

Peter, 17

This type of school would make practicable the tentative scheme of allowing un-academically minded youngsters to try out various jobs before leaving school. Lack of facilities for such enterprises at the present time would be overcome by firms, etc., being compelled by law to reserve places for certain numbers of these 'experimenters' to work side by side with regular employees.

Mary, 16

I should think that the pupil and the school should keep in touch because if the pupil is out of a job the school is something to fall back on. . . . The school would have close ties with local industry, thereby broadening the outlook of teachers and pupils and improving ultimate career opportunities. Teachers, in fact, as part of their training, would be obliged to spend some time in industry

99

and would work with their pupils during their industrial inertia in the summer time.

David, 13

Another point worth raising is that as soon as a pupil leaves school he is immediately cut off from the school. It would be a good idea if the school arranged an evening class for pupils who had different problems about their employment, so that they could go to the classes and discuss these problems with their teachers. I feel this would prevent many pupils from drifting from job to job.

Danny, 15

There should be more co-operation between schools and industry; the latter could try to provide short courses on their premises to show pupils who are interested in a certain business what exactly goes on there, and what particular skills and smaller trades are involved in producing the finished product. . . . For instance, in the cement industry there are jobs involving chemical research, electronics, as well as driving trucks and looking after machinery. Points like this should be made known to pupils in more forceful ways than just talking briefly about them and handing out literature; the pupil must see the trades for himself before making a decision.

John, 16

The girls would do heavy craft, cricket, football and rugby and they would also do their own sports. Girls love the things boys do, and I think that girls can do anything boys can do. Also the boys would do cookery because when they get married and have children it will come in very useful.

Angela, 13

There would be a huge domestic science block for girls and boys – after all, some of the best chefs are men – with equipment for food preparing and cooking, needlework and crafts of all varieties, instructions in child-care and housecraft.

Patricia, 15

Domestic science is outdated. By the time I am a housewife, the cookers I have patiently taken to pieces and washed will be out of date. After all, the ability to clean a home is an instinctive one.

Anne, 17

I would like to see greater emphasis on domestic subjects for girls and home accountancy for boys. Having dropped domestic science in the fourth form for Greek, my knowledge of cookery extends only to cornflake cakes and Welsh rarebit, and yet I shall receive no further cookery lessons before I leave school.

Christa, 16

The present idea that one girl must do Latin while another is fit only for cookery and needlework and, later, marriage, is a common fallacy. An academically bright young wife will undoubtedly find the ability to cook and make clothes a decided advantage, and in the same way I am sure the ability to learn about Latin roots and the derivation of our own language would be beyond few children, and would greatly improve a child's understanding of English and other languages.

Linda, 16

I would like to learn an unusual language, such as Arabic or Chinese, because it is not often a child of my age can do this. It would be very useful and interesting.

Clare, 11

We are forced into Latin, which wastes one seventh of our school career. Why not take German or Russian instead, which could be useful?

Russell, 13

I feel that the present division between arts and sciences is too absolute. Being an arts student I gave up all science at the age of thirteen, too early an age to make such irrefutable decisions. I would like to see more give and take between these camps.

Christa, 16

I myself would like more English and less arithmetic. English is so much more imaginative. The only imagination I use in arithmetic is when I guess the answers.

Melissa, 11

Lessons in voice production would be compulsory, as to be able to talk and converse audibly and fluently is a great asset to anyone.

Stella, 12

Music is great fun but most schools have no music teachers or only a piano teacher. One of the other teachers has to teach the children singing. That teacher is sometimes (and mostly!) a terrible singer who is always off tune before she has got her A. Schools should have (1) a baritone singer to teach boys, (2) a contralto singer to teach girls. There should be more than one piano teacher in a school and other instruments should be taught such as the violin.

Shivaun, 11

No music lessons would be allowed because of the noise that might be produced by those who were inexperienced.

Jane, 15

The histories and biographies of Chopin, Mozart, Beethoven, Handel and other less-known composers should be taught. . . . The interesting and abnormal things that they did during their lives are fantastic and seem to be unbelievable sometimes.

Artists should be employed by each school to train our hands to make images of people, animals and landscapes. In that way children will learn more about art than the school I went to where the only art practised was children drawing pictures of their teachers on the back of their copybooks !

Shivaun, 11

There would be canvasses, oil-paints and turpentine for everyone, and dozens of pottery wheels. Most important of all, there would be tons of clay so that I could fulfil my greatest wish – to model a life-size statue.

Patricia, 15

I would like to go to a school where art, music, sewing, woodwork and sculpture are just as important as any academic lessons, and not treated as once-weekly recreation periods.

Harriet, 14

I would like to see the barriers surrounding art, music, literature and drama broken down. I would like these forms of self-expression to be understood and enjoyed by all, not just a bourgeois minority. This is where I feel that my education fell through.

M. (boy), 17

I feel that all forms of creative art will play a vital part in any attempt to teach pupils to think. While classical art, such as painting a scene from life, teaches nothing, and encourages only the 'born artist', abstract and surrealist art gives the worst pupil the opportunity to experiment with colours and effects. . . . Not that painting alone would be encouraged. All art-forms will produce people who think of the best presentation. Essays and poems are obvious examples. With the development of practically instant photography, a whole new vista of art is developed.

Alan, 16

> **And as for subjects,** less learning by heart
> But more initiative needed, I think –

You could cut out geography, for a start
(Really, *must* we learn where they refine zinc?)

But physics and chemistry need not go,
For they only need bringing up to date;
(They stopped using common pumps long ago,
And bleach powder's use has declined of late!)

Michael, 15

The main thing is to have plenty of gym and games, so that they can use all their energy up and can concentrate on lessons.

Leone, 13

By all means let us continue to practise sport, but I think it would be much more enjoyable if we ceased to regard it as a secondary religion, although I am in a clear minority on this point.

Sharon, 15

Another thing that has always been missing in our schools is the space and money enough for sports to keep children in trim. Many children nowadays live a too comfortable life eating sweets and biscuits, reading trash comics and watching the television. Swimming and life-saving especially should be available and free to every child. Then the mitching child would run to school just for the afternoon swim.

Shivaun, 11

Sports could be chosen. If children wanted to do some other subject instead of it, they could. I would prefer this as I am poor at this subject, but some children live in a world of sport, so much for them. I would like not to play hockey as I am bad at it, but I am quite good at gym and netball. I am bad at tennis but I would like to learn. I wouldn't mind if I played rounders or not. I'm bad at it. Some children have talent at sports; they would find my view hell.

Clare, 11

In the afternoons there would be games. Hockey, football, cricket, tennis, squash and swimming all the year round, but none of them compulsory. Some would go out in groups on expeditions into the country, to a museum or to do social work; some would read or discuss, others draw or have music lessons. When nobody had to do anything, most people would find something of interest from the enormous range of 'extras'. And, of course, dramatics, hobbies and other ex-curriculum subjects would help concentration on the four hour-long lessons a day.

Jeremy, 16

Today, extra-curricular activities are pursued when and where possible in a haphazard way. In the future school, these will be a second part of the day, perhaps from six to eight p.m. each day, during which time the school clubs and societies will operate, and there will be classes where pupils will be able to continue studying subjects which they have had to drop during the normal school time.

Janet, 15

It would be beneficial to establish some definite correlation between School and Enjoyment, and this could be done by setting aside from about four till six o'clock for activities such as: good films followed by discussion, arts and crafts, poetry readings, dramatic activities, chess and ping-pong, musical activities (from Bach to the Beatles), visiting speakers on God, science, travel, etc., and dances on Saturday nights. All these would be staff-advised but pupil-run.

Ian, 16

> **At home some pupils can't do work**
> Because they cannot help but shirk.
> Domestic problems stop some others,
> Noisy children or nagging mothers.
> So after school they could stay behind,
> Perfect conditions for work they would find....

Alan, 16

One Thing that Should not be Forced on Anybody

There was not one voice raised in defence of religious instruction in its present form, or the religious aspect of school assemblies. The religious assembly was widely resented, both because it required apparent assent in a field where there was much dissent or doubt, and also because it was so often an affair of 'familiar soporific droning'. Most of the critics, objecting to having a particular form of religion forced upon them, were far from anxious to leave a gap. In fact, they felt frustrated; they wanted very much to consider the nature of religious experience, to be helped in their search for a philosophy, to be enabled to compare one belief with another. It is not escape from this serious field the children are seeking; it is some better and worthier way into it.

... **mornings of attending school** in a torpid state only to be confronted with that familiar soporific droning of the person leading the service.

Anne, 15

Time is wasted far too much in schools at the moment. The morning assemblies are the main culprits, as they really serve no useful purpose at all. No one listens to the reading, and few sing anything, and therefore, from a religious point of view, it has been absolutely useless. The only useful thing they do is to give the headmaster a chance to give out notices directly to the boys.

Edward, 15

Morning 'prayers' should be optional, with the probable result: no morning prayers.

Ruth, 15

Morning prayers would be continued, but attendance would no longer be obligatory, even for the staff. Although the form of service might be much the same, 'the faithful' would sit at the front with a large space at the back for those who were interested but did not want to commit themselves. Thus we might end the ultimate hypocrisy of four hundred voices lifted in supplication to a God in whom three quarters do not believe.

Rachel, 17

I would like assemblies to become voluntary. This is not because then I could get out of going to assembly, but because religion is one thing that should not be forced on anybody.

Carrol, 15

Religion, like Latin, Greek, Russian, Chinese, music, botany, sports and domestic science, would not be enforced on everyone. God is a personal matter – and even the most ardent Christians should respect this. French schools survive without assemblies and pep talks, so why cannot English schools as well?

Caroline, 14

I would like my school to have a sense of humour and prayers for those who want it; discussions for those who don't.

Harriet, 14

Lessons in R.K. should have discussion as to whether or not God exists. The teacher of R.K. should be broadminded and not insist on believing. We should be taught about other religions and those past, instead of learning the same New Testament happenings every year at the same time. R.K. has not changed since my Victorian grandmother was a teacher.

Ruth, 13

At the moment when an individual is searching for a philosophy of living, he has learnt nothing of the main philosophies and religions of the world at school, and this subject would be taught to replace scripture.

Jeanette, 14

Scripture in its present narrow form would be replaced by a mixture of anthropology and sociology.

Ann, 18

There would be a large department on religion: not teaching you to be a Christian, but discussing all kinds of religions and letting personal beliefs be formed.

Patricia, 15

Scripture should have more time spent finding out about other churches. How and why they differ from each other.

Ruth, 15

I think a school ought to arrange many more discussions between people of different religions, as our religious beliefs play such an important part in our everyday life.

Mary, 14

We have already learnt about Joseph, Jacob, Daniel, etc., and do not want to do so again. Lessons would be far more interesting if we learnt about Gautama Buddha, Islam and Mohammed, of which we know very little. Also, discussions and debates would be of far better value to the pupil than hearing once more about people in the Bible.

S. (boy), 12

Debates would be especially good in religious instruction. Once somebody proposed the motion, 'Heaven does not exist'. I wasn't surprised when most people abstained from voting.

A. (boy), 15

Whan that I was yonge and wente to schole
In oure village, it was evere the reule
That, atte the time of undren, everich day,
All scholere sholde goon for to preye
In the greet halle; and this was oure usage.
And everichon, be they or lite or large,
Took keepe to closen evere fast hir eyen,
And clasp hir hondes, elles if they gan speyen
Or mak a soun, as is a childes wone,
Ful streit weren they chastened, oon and oon.
It seemd me straunge that it sholde so befalle
That Crist, Who in a litel oxes stalle,
For our sakes, a childe yboren was,
Sholde suffere that a litel lamb of His
Be chidde, whan that they did not wel attend.
For this, from childe unto hir lives ende,
Moot thinke it hem that Godde is evere streit,
And nat benigne, al be that He is greet.

I telle yow of this thing, for it seems to me
Greet scathe that aloon the C. of E.
Is the religioun in oure scholes ytoughte,
And eek by hem, who Godde loven noght,
Or but a litel, and do in sondry wyse,
Both goode and badde, techen the Worde of Crist.

So in this competicioun of youre,
Whan that yow ask of oon thing or more
That everich parfait scole sholde han, I seigh
That ther namoor moot alle children preye,
But if they wol; for trew it is to seyen:
No man can maak a yonge persoun to preyen
If they wol not; and eek religioun
Can noot but preestes teche, it is resoun.

Let children lerne of Godde in churches scoles,
And eek in churches lat hem save hir soules.
In scoles of staat, let the goodnesse be taughte
Of man, and al that mannekinde hath ywroghte.

Stephen, 17

This Almighty God

Examinations in their present form are not merely detested – they are also despised. No one, in all these thousand essays, has a word to say for them. The children put their finger on all those aspects of existing examinations that worry many of their elders, but they do not express their criticism in terms of worry and unease, or of cautious curiosity about alternatives. They make their case roundly, with the confidence of victims.

I believe their case is unanswerable. Examinations as they are, the children say, represent the triumph of a distorted view of education, one which sees it as a means of establishing qualifications, of ensuring that children leave school with 'job tickets' (or, of course, fail to do so). An examination of the present type replaces the assessment of the whole work of a child with a verdict on the performance of a few hours. And because that is what it does, it is bound to test what are very often the least living, the least essential parts of a subject : those parts on which certain kinds of question can be asked, and especially those that can be memorized. The children have little doubt that mere memorization is not only (especially under pressure) a dreary and agonizing business, but that it does not deserve to be at the centre of learning, if for no other reason than that much of what you are required to memorize can be more sensibly looked up in books.

Our present examinations also stifle initiative. Bound to a strict syllabus and timetable, a child cannot follow any personal line of inquiry; individual research is out, and few known exams even begin to measure imagination or taste. They favour unoriginality, uniformity of opinion. Again and again they prevent a teacher from following interesting lines of thought that lead beyond the syllabus. The teacher says : 'We haven't time, I'm afraid, to look at that. We simply mustn't waste time if we're to get through the exams.'

Then examinations contribute to that wretched pressure that the children complain of not only in this but in other forms; not the good pressure that comes when you are working fully, eagerly, but that bad pressure that results when you simply have too much to do, of a kind of work in which you do not feel personally engaged, in too little time. One quotation here expresses the not uncommon view that examinations are badly placed, leaving wide spaces of the school year when (because exams provide the only pacemaker) nothing occurs but a wasteful winding down. But the common complaint about exams so far as they influence the use of time within a school is not so much that they are badly programmed as that they give children a damaging sense of being hunted down by time. And anyone who has lived close to a child involved in one of our present examinations knows how true this is, and must have wondered whether this taught a sense of the importance of time or simply a fear of it.

And lastly, existing examinations are felt by children to impose upon them, at several points, painful and uncertain choices between subjects. The outcry about the loss of favourite subjects, the forced making of often deeply regretted and irretrievable choices, comes again and again under this and other headings. Especially many children feel anger because they must drop subjects such as art and music, or practical subjects, for which the timetable made necessary by examinations leaves no room.

Nearly all recognize that there must be assessments of a child's performance. Here and there are found signs that the new C.S.E. (Certificate of Secondary Education) exams are a little more tolerable. But the means of measuring their achievement that children propose would take us well outside the pattern of virtually all present forms of examination. First, they want to be assessed on their entire work, and (as we have seen when they discussed the way they are taught and what they are taught) they want that work itself to be broader in scope, less predetermined, to give far more room for individual research and for practical activity than the present syllabuses give. The present syllabuses cannot provide that room because, in their nature, they are little concerned with the interests of any individual, and find what can be written down easier to test than the fruits of almost all kinds of practical work. And where the conventional element of examination must enter in, the children would like to experiment with new kinds of questioning, requiring new forms of answer. They would like a sensible recognition that the part that books might play in anyone's work cannot possibly be dismissed as mere cheating and copying; so that, instead of having to memorize matter that any intelligent person would expect to check in a text or a work of reference, they believe they should be allowed to use books in any reformed examination. They would also like the exams to be far more concerned with method, with a child's power to make a significant pattern out of given facts, than with the mere putting down of what has been desperately committed to heart.

All this ties in, of course, with their general plea to be given their freedom of the world of learning. Examinations in their present form turn each facet of learning into a little prison, where the individual can put up a stoical show but can hardly hope to be freely himself. Everywhere you turn, as you follow the arguments of these children, you seem to see the source of that absence of freedom they complain of. It lies in inhibited syllabuses, in unadventurous teaching. It also lies in the enormously conservative apparatus of examinations; and if the truth is that there is no single root to the great wrongness of our system of schooling, at any rate the children convince us that there is something about exams that smells very radical indeed.

At the moment we seem to be working merely for the sake of examinations, whereas we should work to satisfy our curiosities.

Patricia, 15

At present our entire secondary educational system is geared to the G.C.E. examinations. Indeed, our grammar schools in particular are nothing more than G.C.E. sausage machines: eleven plus mincemeat is fed in at one end and O- and A-level sausages emerge at the other.

Boy, 13

An examination should be a challenge and something to be enjoyed – not a high-pressurized release from a cramming session from the night before.

M. (boy), 17

'From now, until the end of the examination, there will be silence ... Begin !'

All eyes scan the paper before them, each heart wildly flutters, each brain whirls, all hands are cold and clammy.

No, this is not a concentration camp but a school examination. Each year children are subjected to this violent treatment and then they are expected to develop into intelligent, well-adjusted adults. School examinations as well as being cruel are ridiculous; a child's capacity for learning cannot be measured by such an immoral exercise. Examinations should be abolished, both internal and external.

If school examinations were to be abolished, then it would be necessary for classes to become smaller, in order to allow the teacher to form a closer communication with each pupil. These classes or groups would be co-educational to allow for a natural atmosphere to develop. Each group would not study history, geography, mathematics, English as subjects, but in relationship to life.

But even then someone would undoubtedly discover some other devious device to be exploited and used as a 'job ticket'.

Loraine, 15

The school I'd like would be one whose primary aim was to teach me how to live, and make me a responsible member of society. Today, academic knowledge has become the sole interest of many schools, and few are daring enough to abandon the O-level rat-race for the job of creating thinking, adult individuals.

Christa, 16

Undoubtedly our present tight G.C.E. system has the effect of stifling initiative and personal interest, but is there an alternative to this? I think there is. The recent introduction of C.S.E. was a tangible move in the right direction, but a positive *total* overhaul of the whole system needs to be effected, so that less reliance is placed on memory and more on the other capabilities of children. Teachers and pupils are bogged down, from thirteen and fourteen onwards, in the heavy mire of accumulation of often undigested and unrelated knowledge which can be spewed out as a turgid mark-gaining mess during the examinations. The whole school week becomes geared to the G.C.E. and all extra-curricular activities are forced to prostrate themselves in front of this almighty god. This, surely, is not our ideal British education?

Kenneth, 17

In secondary education today the emphasis is on passing O- and A-levels. Half-educated children emerge from school clutching their exam certificates, having been filled to capacity with information about T. S. Eliot and Plato. They believe themselves to be 'educated'. To some extent they are, I suppose. But are they better equipped to understand and live with their fellow human beings? Moreover, has their education encouraged them to think creatively and originally? Isn't this what education should be about?

Anthony, 18

The present system of examinations (I refer to O- and A-levels) is appalling. Candidates must be judged according to their application to their work throughout the whole course, and *not* to one three-hour cram effort after feverish revision under hysterical conditions. Nothing is left to individual research, imagination or taste, and results of exams prove not the ability of the candidate so much as the temperament of the examiner.

Judith, 18

Having just completed the O-level course, I can say with great feeling that there is too much to do and too little time to do it.

Susan, 16

The examination system must obviously be abolished or at least controlled. One's education becomes a mere soaking up of facts and a long string of exams ... by the end of which time one is accused of being staid and unoriginal. I myself am not escaping

117

from school this year, having just finished O-levels, because in the next two years I am expecting something more from my education. The A-level course seems less pointless and more interesting than the O-level....

Another evil of the exam system is that it means cutting out subjects from one's syllabus at the age of twelve or thirteen. I had only the vaguest idea of what I wanted to do at that time, and although I spent a lot of time trying to make the right decision, I now found I made the wrong one. I am almost completely undomesticated, as there is no time to take academic subjects for O-level and still take practical subjects such as cookery, art or needlework. Inspiring, less conventional subjects like pottery or Chinese are simply not taught. If I had a choice, therefore, I would choose a school where there is no O-level, thus leaving time for other practical subjects and offering boundless scope for capabilities hitherto unnoticed.

Elizabeth, 16

I would not have exams because even though we are told that there is nothing to worry about we still worry and when the results are given out we either get upset or conceited. Exams are a waste of time both to the staff and the pupils.

Angela, 13

If during the course of a French language lesson the teacher should hit on some topic relating to French history, he has to leave the pupils ignorant, as it were, for he hasn't time because 'the exams are coming up soon', and after all he isn't in control of the syllabus! The pupils might know the French language ... but can they say they are educated about France and the French people?

Dermot, 17

In my school, once the exams are over the teachers do not care whether one attends school or not, and nothing is done to help those who might wish to stay on until the end of term. If we had done our exams at Easter we could have a whole term to use on subjects that would help us to live life to the full. After all, the knowledge of nuclear physics and the ability to write a treatise on the abolition of slavery might be very interesting in itself, but it does not come up in everyday conversation very frequently, neither does it equip one to run a home and look after a family. I think the reading of modern and not obscure novels, the appreciation of contemporary art and ideas on how to furnish a room and live on a few pounds a week would be more useful and practical.

Many school leavers, including myself, start this September in a teachers' training college. It is to be hoped that by the time we are fully qualified we will be preparing classes for the G.C.E.s at Easter and not in the summer and, as a result, coping with far larger sixth forms. For students like myself who want to teach, that final term at school could have been devoted to taking the first forms in the school for some of their lessons, thereby giving us a little confidence in our chosen profession, and releasing the teachers for more skilled tasks which they have to perform. Instead, on one day when I went in to school, I was asked would I like to do some weeding?

Carolynne, 18

It is in the sixth form that the boredom which can wreck one's future career and kill one's interest in a particular subject can set in. The cause of this boredom is sometimes too rigid a syllabus, but more often the accent placed on speed. One develops rapidly at this period, especially outside school, but such is the pressure of work that little time can be set aside for discussion, which is a necessity for one's basic understanding of a subject, and nearly all one's time is taken up by the cataloguing and absorbing of facts.

David, 18

In the first place I'd better say that I'm beginning to doubt the usefulness of any exam system – I don't see how three years' work can be summed up in three hours. Exams ultimately remove most of the pleasure you might have been able to take from your work. Their results seem horribly dependent on the mood of the examiner – it would, I should imagine, make rather a large difference to your result whether he marked your papers first or last, for instance. But I am certain that the present syllabus is worse than useless. Here are the papers (with their marks) taken for French: dictation (20 marks), oral (30 marks), prose (translation from English into French) (50 marks), essay (in French) (50 marks), unseeen (two translations from French into English) (100 marks), literature (100 marks). For literature, four books must be studied; in the paper you have to write four commentaries (on one passage from each book) and two essays – all in three hours. This means that to do a good literature paper you must do more work on it than on all the other papers put together. That fact speaks for itself.

First, let's consider language and the question: When do you know a language? I suggest that it lies in being able to understand, use and speak it even without knowledge of your own language. In other words, when I look at a passage of French, I should be able to understand it without translating it; when I speak or express my ideas in French, this expression should be spontaneous, without need of translation. Above all, knowing French is not necessarily being able to translate from English into French and vice versa, although they have some part in it. So the most important papers in the language section should be the oral and the essay, which encourage the spontaneous expression of French. As you see, they are the least important.

Now for literature. I hope you will excuse the long and horribly involved metaphor which follows. If I were studying a machine, I would not remove four cogs from it and study them individually, detached from the machine to which they belong; I would, perhaps, study these cogs in their context. I would examine their relation and their function in the machine. The machine is French literature; the four cogs the four books we study minutely, painfully and uselessly. If I am studying a book by Molière, I ought to be able to place it in its social, historical, literary and artistic context; I should study it not only in the light of Molière's other work but in the light of the social and political pressures and artistic and philosophical ideas that formed it. A work of art may be universal in its application, but it is temporal in its expression; to understand it completely I must understand the epoch that formed it. A knowledge of four books does not make up a knowledge of French literature; a study of four books, and their authors, taken in their literary and historical context, may at least help to.

R. (boy), 17

To be happy at his work a student must be doing the work he wants to do; he should not be rigidly restricted by the organization of the tuition, the exam syllabus or indeed university entrance requirements. Thus the education would be as flexible as possible. The basic A-level courses would be retained, but within a basic syllabus framework the student would select the lectures he wished to attend, therefore making his work more personal and ultimately more valuable. Students would be able to choose their A-levels from a wider range of subjects so that their education was more accurately aligned with their careers or university degrees. Most courses would be spread over three years, for in addition to their three specific subjects, students would study for a general A-level which would consist of anything the student wished, but he would have to show interest in subjects other than his A-levels. Thus, beside the fact that all lectures would be open to all students, with such subjects as philosophy, politics and psychology available, the yawning arts/science schism would close considerably.

Simon, 18

No one has adequately stated the function of a school, which must be to produce a complete human being useful to society. This is by no means the present aim of the majority of schools in this country: their aim can be summed up in one word – qualifications. The universities, hypocritically claiming that they do not want narrow specialists, limit the last three years of a student's school life to the exclusive study of three subjects. Arts entrants leave school qualified in English, French and History. They have not studied any other subjects since they were fifteen or so. This is not the fault of the schools, but of a system which demands three good A-level passes before it will admit anyone to its universities. It is a paradoxical fact that the grammar schools are producing people patently unfitted for life in society, while secondary modern schools are providing the happy, balanced people of this country....

Obviously this concentration [on a few subjects] is a job for the universities, not the grammar schools. A student who at eighteen has a good knowledge of six or seven subjects has not been forced to limit himself to three at an age when he is totally incapable of choosing. If he wishes to go to university he will choose a course in the subject or subjects which he has enjoyed most.... The system described would not mean a lowering of standards, catch-phrase of many reactionaries, as the onus would be placed where it belongs, on the university.

Peter, 17

As most exams seem to be testing one's ability to memorize facts, I think they should be changed to those testing one's actual understanding of the subject. Obviously, some basic facts have got to be known, but apart from that I think exams should have more of a practical side to them. This applies particularly to science subjects. Maths, for example, could be made far more interesting by doing some practical work instead of eternally working through textbook examples. The reason many people dislike maths is because it is so boring. For lessons to have a more practical side it is necessary to have a great deal of space, which is what is greatly lacking at the moment. Schools will *have* to be rebuilt to provide this extra space.

Ursula, 15

If a new teaching technique is to be introduced, the system of exams must be changed. Exams cannot be abolished, because they provide the means by which an examiner may grade the ability of a pupil in a subject. If exams involved a short written paper on a wide theme such as 'Science in the Home' for example, an interview and practical work, this would abolish learning by heart where a large syllabus was involved. Once the syllabus had been replanned, pupils could work more independently. A third or a half of the allotted lesson time on a subject could be spent on individual research with the help of television, radio and films from a special library. Then the pupils would meet together and hold discussions with the teacher and ask questions on their findings.

Lorraine, 15

I think that it is necessary to have some way of measuring a pupil's ability. Examinations are a faulty method, since examination technique, including the ability to write fast, is of paramount importance. Examinations would be fairer if a greater number of papers were set and different types of question asked: e.g. those needing one-word answers and those requiring an imaginative approach.

Janet, 16

All the term work will be heeded,
Thus exams will not be needed.

Ruth, 16

The mind is forced to be filled with disjointed bits of knowledge which are reeled off in exams. It is very rare that anyone needs this complete knowledge stored away, for they can, if they need it, look it up in a book. The most important thing is that they must know which book to look it up in. Exam candidates today should be given a set of questions, a set time and be allowed to wander around a library and find the correct answers. . . .

It should be realized that children need to be prepared for their lives and not taught about the lives of the teachers.

Lynda, 16

Examinations would not necessitate the cramming of large stores of knowledge into a tightly packed brain a few weeks or even days beforehand. Rather, they would be an examination of method, practising the ability to reflect soundly and swiftly on a problem, such as reconciling different points of view on a subject, and reaching a well-considered conclusion.

Elizabeth, 17

Against All Laws of Nature

It is girls who are most vehemently opposed to single-sex schools. It is also a minority of girls who would cling to them. The view of the majority, of both sexes, is perfectly simple. Life is bi-sexual, and schools would be well advised not to pretend otherwise. A price is paid, ranging from shyness to unnatural appetite, by those who enter the world from a single-sex school. As for the famous argument that girls and boys distract one another from school work – let the teacher recognize that, they say, as merely another, perfectly legitimate, challenge to his professional skill.

I find the separation of the sexes at the age of eleven or less both archaic and harmful. For girls who go to a single-sex school and who are not endowed with elder brothers, the male sex becomes a sex either to fear and avoid or to seek, find and seduce – all of which makes ordinary, day-to-day relationships with the opposite sex difficult in the extreme.

Elizabeth, 16

I hated boys when I was a fat, introverted eleven-year-old, was quite happy to be segregated into a girls' grammar school. But now, having sampled also a girls' comprehensive school and a co-educational Scottish school abroad, I am certain that all schools must be co-educational. The old tale of the sexually aware adolescent being distracted in class must be only a challenge to the educators, to make their classes interesting enough in their words to forget their boyfriends until breaktime.

Marilyn, 17

In an all-girls' school, things go all right for a couple of days, but after that it seems a dull lifeless building. It's not the girls who have changed or the teachers or the building. The girls want different company. Boys are lively and they make everyone around them like it too.

Sandra, 15

It would have to be mixed, as where in life are not male and female working together? In prison? In a monastery?

Paul, 15

The idea of separating girls and boys at the age of eleven when they have been together at school for six years and then thrusting them together again at eighteen (or whenever they leave school) seems quite nonsensical to me. During this 'time of separation', one tends to come to regard members of the opposite sex as something different or special, something to be encountered out of one's daily routine instead of being part of everyday life.

Edna, 16

I see no point in separating the sexes – after all, they have to know the horrid truth about each other one day, so why not at secondary school? Anyway, one-sex schools seem to be against all laws of nature.

Ruth, 15

I choose a co-ed comprehensive because at such a school one would be able to meet many kinds of youngsters from many kinds of background and not be uneasy with the opposite sex. In other words, enter the social world at an early age.

Louis, 15

Many boys and girls are separated when they are eleven from the opposite sex and remain so until they go to college, university or work. And when they finally meet, neither of them knows what to say or how to say it without offending the other.

Valerie, 16

One last thing, the playgrounds. These are for both girls and boys. They may fight, but if a boy cannot be allowed to be with a girl, then when he grows up, he shall be downright shy of them (when first meeting a girl), or be rotten to them.

Antony, 13, and Christopher, 13

That Race of Strange Beings

'The primary tool of education – the teacher – is far from perfect.' This grave verdict by a fourteen-year-old girl will be no news to anyone, and certainly not to teachers; but, alas, the indictment of the profession as one heaps it together from the writings of these children amounts to more than a statement of their ordinary human imperfection. That child herself accuses her own teachers of sometimes inflicting 'cruel mental punishment'; of being remote from the world of their pupils; of being makers of foolish and frustrating rules. A handful of essays saying such things might be dismissed as no evidence at all, but here are hundreds that make the same complaints, until a most unhappy picture is built up. Of course, grievance often speaks louder than satisfaction, and no doubt many good teachers missed being described because their excellence made them invisible. But it really won't do to try to soften the effect of it all. At the very least it must be said that a great many teachers are found singularly unsatisfactory by those they teach. And the main charges are made so insistently, and by so many, and tie in so closely with the general pattern of criticism, that they certainly require the most serious consideration.

The general theme is that relations between teachers and their pupils are poor, where they are not downright bad. It isn't simply that teachers can be insulting, rude and cruel, though such words are used rather more often than is comfortable. It isn't only that many are found to be impatient, unable to recognize the simple importance of happiness within the school community, lacking in enthusiasm. Of far more consequence, and embracing these other complaints, is the charge that they are teachers first, aloof authoritative persons, and ordinary companionable human beings a long way behind, if at all.

The burden of these essays is that children want an end to the old remoteness between teacher and pupil. One child suggests that the origins of that sort of barely friendly relationship might lie in a teacher's training. The child's sister, herself a trainee teacher, had said that students in a college of education were treated 'like kids'. It is impossible to deny that this is the attitude in some colleges. The student teacher, if only because he is usually going from school back to school, needs to be helped to become a full adult, and petty rules at college, tutors who treat the student *de haut en bas* prevent this from happening. So when the young teacher enters the schools, he cannot be flexible and relaxed in his relationships with children; he can only reproduce the attitudes he has been taught (by implication if not directly). To be at ease with children in the way they wish, you have to be very grown up, and to have had experience yourself in the making of relationships that subtly balance authority with sympathy. So far, so bad : there is a vicious circle, from school to college of education back to school, which goes on repeating a poor and unhelpful pattern of human relationships – the teacher afraid to relax, simply because he does not know how to do this without losing his authority; the child longing to break through, to find in this person who is so important to him more than the frosty player of a narrow role. But the accusation goes further still. Teachers, it is claimed, also have little time for the opinions of their pupils. They brush such opinions aside, ignore them, or simply never elicit them. The adolescent, in particular, they regard as a 'dangerous freak', a serious potential nuisance. They fail to recognize the importance of praise and encouragement.

The picture is very clear. As a former teacher, let alone as a former pupil, I recognize its truth. Often in their training, often too in the atmosphere of the system they enter, teachers are encouraged to think of their relationship with their children in limited terms. It really is a vicious circle. The nature of most of the teaching, thought of as the transfer of a set body of knowledge from teacher to child rather than as a creative contact open to surprise, easily sets a limit to the teacher's role. Because such teaching leads so often to boredom and frustration, the children (with all that is liveliest in them, their curiosity and half-grown opinions as well as their sense of fun, shut out of the classroom) fidget and fool, whereupon the teacher sets even fiercer, frostier limits to his relationship with them. With the years, and when you've learnt the tricks, it becomes terribly easy to play this narrow role, never to reach out to the children, never to permit any really open contact. Those children who in these essays see the connexion between the need for a new kind of teaching and a new kind of teacher – especially those who see that the new teaching would *produce* the new teacher – are surely right. The teacher tends to be narrow and limited, and to exhibit all those qualities of personality that naturally result, because the aims of teaching itself are on the whole narrow and limited. I have drawn up a list of the qualities the children wish their teachers had, and once they are set out one sees that a new order of teaching is being described as much as a reformed type of teacher. They should be understanding, the children say, and patient; should encourage and praise wherever possible; should listen to their pupils, and give their pupils a chance to speak; should be willing to have points made against them, be humble, kind, capable of informality, and simply pleasant; should share more activities with their children than they commonly do, and should not expect all children to be always docile. They should have a conscience about the captive nature of their audience; should attempt to establish links with parents; should be punctual for lessons; enthusiastic within reason; should not desert a school lightly; should recognize the importance to a child of being allowed to take the initiative in school work; and above all, should be warm and personal. It is quite difficult to be all these things within the present pattern of schooling, within the enclosed classrooms, the enclosed curriculum, under pressure from examinations, and in an atmosphere in which so commonly the teacher, representative of a sometimes rather desperately respectable profession, cannot bring himself to accept and value the awkward, gay, intensely critical, iconoclastic, discontented and often shapelessly unconfident character of the modern adolescent. It is really very difficult to be the teacher the children desire, without enormous changes in the whole system. But any link in a vicious circle has some power to break the circle, and teachers can hardly fall back on a plea of impotence.

If, to any teacher, all this should seem a tall order, and the children's criticisms of their teachers to be an outburst of irresponsible impertinence, it must be said finally that a great many, other than those quoted here, coupled their criticism with two stout statements : first, that they couldn't imagine the circumstances in which a teacher might be replaced by machines; and second, that teachers were of enormous importance to them, as being among the most influential human beings they were likely ever to encounter. And often enough such affirmations were accompanied by a very practical statement of the children's support: they believed firmly that teachers should be better paid.

Recently many people have theorized on – and actually produced – the most amazing devices to aid education. They seem to forget that the primary tool of education – the teacher – is far from perfect. Most educationists have no idea of the amount of cruel mental punishment (such as heavy sarcasm, which the pupil is in no position to reply to) that is used by teachers, or of the poor relationship between pupils and staff. Maybe there are exceptions, but they are rare.

I believe there is a definition of a teacher that goes something like this: 'A person who tries to impart knowledge to his pupils, even when they are listening to pop records, and, when he finds that he is not succeeding, sits and listens to them with his pupils.' It takes quite a stretch of my imagination to see any of our teachers doing this – and I fear they would be laughed at if they tried. (Such as a teacher who was an object of amusement for several weeks after admitting to watching *Top of the Pops* to 'keep up with what you like'. It was commendable of her to watch it and, I suppose, permissible to mention it, but why she had to give her reason for watching it never fails to amaze me.)

Teachers also make rules. They are practical, business-like rules, carefully designed to squash the faintest flicker of originality. (What I want to know is how on earth were artists, writers, etc., educated to escape this crushing type of restriction?) Such rules as 'knee length ankle socks must not be worn', taking a ring off a girl that she had worn all her life (admittedly returning it, but with strict instructions never to wear it in school again) and giving a 'late detention' to a girl who was late for afternoon school, but had been choosing a book in the school library – two minutes' walk away from the classroom – until the bell went. These rules are not only restricting, but petty.

Elen, 14

I would like to have teachers that are strict, but not overstrict, who are feared by some and respected by all. An example of this is a teacher at grammar school who for the first two years was a terror to all small boys. He would seemingly appear from nowhere and pounce on any wrong-doer. After that, he would still be strict, but everyone respected him and knew that he was really a fair man. Nowadays, that type of teacher is becoming obsolete, only to be replaced by over-dressed arrogant men who use long words to embarrass and trap people.

Barry, 16

Some teachers say insulting things to their pupils with a leer in their voices. Some teachers, however, say such things but do not mean them. The former, I think, should not be teachers, but the latter are tolerable.

Louis, 14

The teachers would be understanding and have patience. I find myself getting into nervous flaps with teachers who have a hot temper.

Clare, 11

I think the teachers should encourage us instead of giving us a most boring lecture on what we have done wrong. The teacher only wastes his breath. Nobody listens. These lectures are, in my opinion, inclined to make you believe that you cannot go through with what you have set your mind on, i.e. exams. I have myself experienced this. When a teacher praises you for your good work you want to carry on with it and do better.

Rachel, 15

The pupils should be given more chance to speak and the teacher should be given a chance to listen.

Susan, 13

The fault with a lot of schools today is that teachers are not prepared to listen. There is a teacher at our school who is very keen on discussions until somebody makes a point which she is unable to explain, and she gets angry and tells us to sit down. I think that's the attitude of most teachers today. They don't mind discussing various topics as long as it ends up with them being able to prove a point to you and not the other way.

Lyne, 15

I know that in lessons which drag, people file their nails, gaze blankly into space and daydream. This would have to end. The staff would have to have enough control to keep the class in order, but enough liveliness and ability to make the lesson interesting. The pupils should be treated as people, and not as if they had no right to breathe in the same air as the staff. ... When children cannot understand what the subject is about, they naturally lose interest in it. They feel it isn't worth bothering about and are usually afraid to ask a question in case they are laughed at. In our form, mathematics is always like this, and the teacher, instead of asking people where they go wrong, attends to the star pupils. This is not the way, she should know just when to stop for a time and explain.

Eveline, 14

Respect for the pupil is just as important as respect for the teacher, because after a young person's opinion has been disregarded three or four times the young person may never express an opinion again.

Sheila, 15

A teacher can be very rude and cruel to a child, but any objection on his part is treated as impertinence. Education is a search after the truth, and to find the truth one must be humble. This is impossible if teachers are too proud to admit when they are wrong.

Janet, 16

Each morning, for the minimum of four years, a young sensitive person becomes part of a system which cannot accept him as an individual. Teachers dismiss individual actions as a calamitous breach of school regulations. This person is then accepted as an unequal. Rejected and observed with guarded curiosity – in fact, a freak. A freak, however, who is attempting to endanger the security of their society, and who must be evicted from the system it cannot adhere to.

The attitude of the teacher towards the older pupil, a pupil whose intellectual abilities are developing at a much quicker rate than ever before, is one of condescending neutrality. He is unable to attribute thinking faculties to his pupil outside the boundaries of the syllabus. Thus, there evolves a conflict between the teacher and the pupil concerning the liberty of the mind. The young mind seeks to exist beyond the inflexible limits of the classroom, but is trapped by the intransigent will of the teacher. The mental resources of the pupil are dissipated by the constant struggle for his emotional and intellectual freedom. His whole system is discordant with the system he is obliged to accept. Eventually the one is forced to accept the ruling of the majority. The pupil is no longer capable of imbibing any subsequent knowledge. The positive vibrancy of the initial persona is negated.

Cay, 17

In primary schools, there is a friendly relationship between teacher and pupil and the children feel at ease with their teacher. I think this part of our school does not need improving or modernizing at all. The children are happy doing things, not just writing them. Do not try and improve on this, you may spoil it!

Jane, 13

We are always being told that school is really like a big family, and I think that they should try and get a better atmosphere if they want us to think like that, because I think that school is too formal. I don't mean because we call the teachers 'Sir' or 'Madam', but because there usually seems to be a barrier between us and the teachers, which doesn't seem to be there when we have students teaching us.

Carole, 14

... **attempts at fraternizing** with members of staff have so far led to rebuffs and an attitude I can only describe as 'stuffy'. A pleasant atmosphere doesn't cost a penny and, provided it were not carried to excess, could not fail to do some good.

Sharon, 15

The fact is that a school contains two societies – that of the pupils and that of the teachers. Whilst this state of affairs exists, it is difficult for each party to understand the other, and therefore respect wears thin. If the two parties could mix at all times during school hours – teachers take their milk with the children, join in school activities such as sport, dramatics, school magazine and so on, and out-of-school activities such as helping mentally handicapped children – then I feel sure that both sides would begin to show a certain respect for each other. After all, by discussing problems of method with the pupils themselves, and generally joining in with their society, a greater understanding between the two generations will occur. Corporal punishment and school rules could then be dispensed with, any trouble being greeted with general distaste by members of the joint society.

Richard, 17

Many of the pupils of the future will not accept, as many of us did and still do, the dictatorial methods of teachers who regard the classrooms as their own little despotic kingdoms. We sit down at desks and accept, for the most part, what we are told. In the future, discussions will, I feel sure, take the place of mere instruction. But could this really be carried out successfully in the very cramped atmosphere of a 1967 classroom ... at times more akin to an 1867 prison cell? No! In the future, rooms will have to be provided, comfortable to the extent of being an extension of home. (Then truly the teachers would be *in loco parentis*.) An almost informal atmosphere would prevail, one in which the teacher and pupil would be equals.

Dermot, 17

Schools would not be schools without teachers. Those great beings so full of knowledge, wisdom . . . and old age. I admit in the last few years the staff is becoming younger. People say the older you are the wiser you are. They forget the older you are the less patient you become with youth – that noisy bunch of hooligans who insist on running in the corridors and scribbling 'United for the Cup !' and 'I love Steve' on the blackboard. But all work and no play makes Jack a dull boy, and laughter is harmless and helpful. Once the class has let off steam at the beginning of the lesson, they will settle down to work better. In the end everyone is happy, and happiness is a valuable commodity that some schools forget to include on the syllabus.

Jennifer, 15

The teachers, especially head teachers, should be nearer the age of the children, especially in secondary schools. If they were, they would be able to understand our point of view, why we disagree with their opinions on rules, uniform, etc., and not just say : 'Don't be insolent, take a detention'.

Irene, 15

The teachers would be young and understanding, the headmistress would be middle-aged, a wise, kind person, married, and loved by us all. She would look after us devotedly, supervising the teachers and giving sensible advice. She would be a person with a knowledge of all subjects, a woman of the world.

Gillian, 13

. . . **teachers that were old fashioned** would be got rid of. Old-fashioned teachers are the type that give out lines to a class that makes the slightest noise; they also regard the pupils' opinions as cheek.

Ruth, 13

The teachers would not be over forty-five years old or under twenty-five, because teachers over forty-five are usually a bit lax and old fashioned and very young teachers usually have difficulty in enforcing discipline and keeping order.

Margaret, 14

Teachers I think should have extra training to be able to control a class. I know we teenagers can be really spiteful, but I think it is partly the teacher's fault. If he or she had a certain amount of discipline, there would not be so many riots as there are in our school. I think if a teacher cannot control a class, the teacher should either give the job up, go away for disciplinary training, or become a nervous wreck.

Rachel, 15

The school I would like is one where there are young teachers, because I find that most teachers who have been teaching for a long time try to model schools on what it was like in their own schooldays when it was not as enjoyable as today.

Mark, 12

The teachers would be very young so that they would understand you more. There would be only one old person, that would be the cook. She would be very fat and jolly, with a loud laugh. The food that she cooks would be home-made and not dehydrated like some schools have.

Janis, 14

I admit that if all the teachers were oldish men it would be a bit rough on the physical education teacher, although a small fat middle-aged man as a P.E. instructor would suit me perfectly.

Katherine, 12

At present education is split between two separate establishments: the family group and school, with the family concentrating on the social, intellectual and religious aspects, and the school on the academic side. I would like to see these more fully integrated, and this could be achieved by radically broadening the responsibilities of the school. I believe the root of the trouble in the present system is an almost complete breakdown of interpersonal communications within the school. Why is this?

Because the teacher has been trained with the wrong priorities in mind. He is treated by his pupils primarily as a teacher and only secondly, if that, as a person. This is fundamentally wrong, and is so because of a weakness in the teacher and not, as one would like to suppose, in the pupils. To discover why, I asked my sister who is at teacher training college how she was treated by the staff there. 'Like kids.'

How can anyone rationally suppose that when she is fully trained, she will contradict what she has indirectly been taught, and adjust herself to her pupils' level, to communicate with them and consequently educate them properly? Ask any child what his favourite subject is, and the chances are it will be one in which he has, or has had, a teacher whom he liked. In other words, teachers should be trained to communicate personally with their pupils, so that education follows on naturally and easily.

I would like to be taught by someone who has either a university degree plus one year's teacher training or three or four years teacher training, but in either case has mainly got the job for his personality and ability to inspire.

A second reason for the breakdown of interpersonal communications within the school: because schools are compulsory. Now this is a very difficult question, and the consequences of having optional schooling could be quite disastrous, as our culture is not ready for it yet. I would like to have some escape system whereby I could leave a class when I felt I could gain no more benefit from it: i.e. when my interest and concentration were exhausted. This would put pressure on the teachers to hold the interest of their class, because at the moment I suspect (and I may be entirely wrong) that some, being assured of the presence of their class, do not put all they could into their lessons. It would also save valuable time at present spent staving off Bedlam caused by uninterested minority groups in the classroom, as they would soon leave to go home or spend their time more profitably on a subject they like.

Some definite time, say an afternoon a week, should be set aside on the teacher's timetable specifically for the purpose of visiting parents. Besides obliging the teacher to take an individual interest in each of his pupils, it would complete the parent–teacher–child relationship which could only be for the better.

Ian, 16

I know one thing that I would make a rule, it's to have all the teachers meet our mothers at school, only if it's once a term it would be the best thing which ever happened.

K. (boy), 13

One of the first radical changes I should advocate would be the abolition of colleges of education for teacher training. Teaching would be reorganized on the following basis. Only heads of subject departments and headmasters would receive specialized training at full-time colleges. Other teaching would be a version of conscription, each member of society would be asked to contribute a certain proportion of his time to take a course and teach and educate others in his particular skill. In this way those at places of education would receive fresh information from a variety of people, learning at the same time to accept people with their own enthusiasms and shortcomings. This system would also help ease the shortage of teachers and the constant bickering about wages and hours.

Mary, 16

Teachers would have to be punctual for lessons. Sometimes a whole lesson is wasted because a teacher is late.

Janet, 14

The staff would go on a compulsory course every five years to ensure that they know about the latest developments in both education generally and their own subjects.

Janice, 16

Teachers should be more enthusiastic about their subject. There is nothing worse than sitting in a lesson knowing full well that the teacher is dying to get rid of you and rush back to the staff-room to have her cup of tea.

Ruth, 15

The staff would have to be prepared not to leave in the middle of the year, as they seem to – at least, in my present school.

Janet, 16

I attend what is known as a direct grant school, which is in my opinion a public school which has fallen into bad times and is helped by the government. In fact it is run like this with the bourgeois air of a public school. It has a high academic standard and a highly trained staff headed by an excellent but maybe disliked headmistress. The school is in beautiful surroundings with good facilities for work, the arts and sport. It sounds like the dream school, maybe, but its outside looks are deceptive.

There is a fundamental spirit missing of wanting to learn, and though this may sound the fault of the pupils I would think not as they are all of fairly high intelligence and have all gone through a special exam to get in and are usually willing to learn as most children are. We are not stimulated in any way to find things out for ourselves or to experiment in any way with our lessons, the general theory being 'as long as you can do it, it doesn't matter if you don't understand'. The teachers, though they have all been through a rigorous training and are filled to the top with child psychology, are cold and impersonal at all times. When I was younger I got the impression that lessons were delightful things which made our knowledge grow and were to be looked forward to and enjoyed. Teachers were friends who could be talked to and confided in if you did not want to talk to your parents about something.

But as I have described, my ideas of this are shattered. Of course, this is not so for everybody, for there are schools where teachers are called by their Christian names and have an excellent relationship with their pupils. They can both talk freely and easily to each other about the child's problems, and the teacher can guide the child as he or she thinks. This is what is missing so terribly in my school – the lack of stimulance and relationships with teachers.

We ought to be able to do more for ourselves, not always have so much supervision, be given much more responsibility. If we were, maybe we would not behave as stupidly as we sometimes do. If we were given work to do and could do it alone and present the finished article well done to the teacher without being told what to do, the standard would be higher as in a school like mine everyone has a high sense of achievement. There is a certain satisfaction in handing in a piece of well-written work as I will feel when I post this entry that I have done alone without supervision and without being told.

As for the relationship with teachers, that needs a joint effort on the part of the teacher and pupil. If the teachers would take some interest in their jobs and work for them and not just think of teaching the little brats as the best method of making their bread and butter, the pupils I am sure would respond a great deal better and would respect the teachers a lot more for taking an interest and helping them with their problems. I often feel acutely embarrassed if a problem has been gone over a few times and I still do not understand it and ask the teacher if she could possibly explain it to me. She will then sigh and say, 'I've explained it twice and you ought to have listened.' This is typical of the teachers' 'couldn't-care-less-about-the-pupils' attitude which is found throughout my school.

So basically the school I would like must have a happy spirit with plenty of stimulance for learning to live and work, and good relationships with teachers.

Monica, 14

The first step must surely be to raise teachers' salaries by at least fifty per cent to recruit top class personnel to the profession. And the only means of doing this is by offering salaries commensurate with their responsibility in shaping the hopes of tomorrow and competitive with those offered by industry. Furthermore it is imperative that teaching staff be relieved of extra duties.

Sidney, 15

If children are to be taught solely by stereotyped machines, are we not in grave danger of producing mechanical, stereotyped children? The place of the human, individual teacher must always remain secure to provide a contrast to machine-teaching.

Paul, 13

I feel there is nothing like a teacher's enthusiasm for his subject to make learning a pleasure, and I am sure that a computer cannot show enthusiasm.

Jeremy, 13

I would use computers in my ideal school as I feel that this would cancel out any teachers' errors and this would mean that no child's education would be impeded by a teacher who is slow or not experienced.

Beverley, 14

Modern equipment? To me, it's sheer poppycock. We want intelligent teachers and not machines. It is the poor doctor who hides behind a whole gamut of patent drugs.

Cosette, 17

Please, Lord, ease our teachers' lot by giving them more pay, which would also mean that those who enter the profession would not do so only as a last resort. This would lead to better teachers, and would perhaps lessen the number of those who dither in confusion for the first part of the lesson – clearing up from the previous form; finding where we are; recapping on the last lesson – and groan miserably that: 'We'll never finish the course at this rate' for the rest of it, and then expect us to do at home, alone, the work which they should have done with us in class, ensuring a late night followed by a morning when, if we reach school at all, we miss enough work to guarantee us another late night. ...

May that race of strange beings, the Teaching Profession, flourish! Though teachers are ridden with idiosyncrasies and varied prejudices, it is in observing their little foibles that we learn to recognize and to control our own; we learn that other people see things in a different light from ourselves, and we learn to respect their right to do so. A computer could not teach us to live.

Anne, 17

A Sore Point

School uniform was a major theme, but the principal arguments can be represented by a small number of quotations. Among girls, fantasy tended to reign, often side by side with a quite moderate text, and few resisted the temptation to submit sketches of their ideal uniforms : ranging from mini-shifts to conventional gym-slips in improbable shades. A largeish minority were against uniform of any kind, seeing the demand that they wear it as the worst of all the school's arbitrary rules, and as a particularly intolerable attempt to make 'children' of them. Usually they argued that the imposition of a uniform throughout school life made it difficult for a child to develop any dress sense. The majority were in favour of some sort of uniform, accepting that it was a leveller, and that it saved them from the strain of sartorial rivalries. But they wanted uniform to have at least some connexion with fashion, and girls especially wanted to remove from it those qualities that, they seemed to suspect, were designed to make them safely sexless. Many thought there should be consultation between the interested parties – school, parents, children – to work out a compromise that would be agreeable to the young without promoting actual apoplexy among their elders.

It is still seriously thought that if we all wear the same type of clothes, we'll all go round thinking our parents earn the same amount of money. Pupils should be allowed to dress in the manner in which they feel comfortable, and any good head teacher will use his own discretion in tactfully censuring the odd exhibitionist.

Roy, 15

I go to a school which has a uniform, and I am glad it does. There is no problem deciding what to wear each morning, no class distinction at school, and no one trying to look better than the person next to them, everyone is equal.

Jane, 15

After eleven years of being buttoned up inside a regimentally enforced school uniform, on leaving school the child will doubtless abandon all sense of colour and taste in the joy of being free from it. If, however, the child is given eleven years in which to develop a taste in clothes, he will feel himself adult and act in an adult fashion.

Christa, 16

I am all for uniforms. If pupils were allowed free choice in dress, richer children would tease the poorer ones about their clothing. Girls would want to show off a new 'mod' outfit, but this might get spoilt after one day at school. I should like a modern dress, with pockets, in a warm, inexpensive material for winter, and the same in cotton for summer. Skirts are so hard to keep in good shape, mothers hate ironing white shirts and girls despise wearing ties. A dress is less expensive and far more comfortable.

Sheila, 15

There would be no school uniform at all and the pupils would wear whatever they wanted. I am sure they would soon learn which clothes were suitable for school and which were not – even if it caused several members of the staff frequent nightmares wondering what Jane or Jimmy would be wearing tomorrow. Everybody has to form his own individual dress sense, and how can this be done if everybody is forced to dress exactly alike for most of the day?

Ruth, 15

Let us continue to wear a uniform. It no doubt inhibits our personalities by depriving us of a means of self-expression, and has grave psychological repercussions, but it prevents nervous stress,

146

occasioned by being unable to decide what to wear. Besides, the effects of multi-coloured classes on members of staff must be considered.

Anne, 17

A great number of people have put forward the suggestion that when everyone is dressed differently, one becomes too absorbed in clothes to work. It is much easier to work when you feel comfortably dressed, and very rarely are school uniforms comfortable.

Angela, 15

Uniform has to go, or be radically reformed. While many boys look quite dashing in uniform, girls merely look de-sexed and shabby. It lowers the morale no end and produces a kind of work-house atmosphere. I am not against uniform on principle – I would just like to move with the time and be reasonably attractive.

Elizabeth, 16

I remember hearing about a school which asked pupils to sub-mit suitable designs and ideas. This arrangement successfully com-bined the pupils' ideas of fashion, and the adults' ideas of respect-ability and neatness. This would be a suitable arrangement for my school.

S. (boy), 12

Uniform is a sore point with many girls. We come in all shapes and sizes and a dress that suits one hangs like a sack on another. So why not have two or possibly three patterns to choose from, and easily obtainable in the shops? Some of us aren't so well off and expensive dresses, blouses, skirts and unnecessary ties make a difference at home. Blazers are rather a nuisance, too. Too hot really for summer, yet impractical for rainy weather. Anoraks are smart and warm at the right time, cool at the right time.

Nina, 14

The uniform would be of simple structure. One loose, light, comfortable shift-type dress would be much more attractive, if not smarter, than the standard uniform. However are we expected to act 'lady-like' and 'feminine' in shoes that are seemingly adapted from clogs, a uniform like that of a military training school? Surely everyone is entitled to some comfort each day?

Valerie, 14

The school should not keep to the same uniform Lady Mabel Ramsbottom-Smith designed out of the goodness of her heart some twenty years ago.

Jennifer, 13

One of the Main Grumbles

If school meals are ever widely improved, children will lose one of their best jokes and most beloved grouches. But it is clear from the evidence of these essays that they would endure the loss gladly. Given their attachment to the joke, there can't be any doubt that in a great many schools the meals are still badly cooked and indifferently served. The chief pleas come again and again, and are all represented here : not only for good cooking, but for varied menus, some say in the size of the meal on any particular occasion, the avoidance of banal or eccentric combinations of dishes; an opportunity to choose among alternatives; and a pleasant environment in which to eat.

As you know, most school food is poor.

Clare, 11

Meals provide one of the main grumbles at my school, very often the cooking is unsatisfactory and the food is not very good anyway – but as soon as a governor comes and stays for dinner, the meal is a vast improvement on what we usually get. I would like to go to a school where the standard of cooking and food are so good that nobody grumbles, and there is the choice of an alternative meal.

Alan, 16

Basic school dinners should be avoided as the food (and management) is usually disgusting. (The teachers avoid the school dining hall but ruthlessly force the pupils to eat the 'nourishing food' which has been cooked hours before in the city centre welfare kitchens.)

Carol, 16

School meals are ghastly affairs, which always cause disturbances among pupils and adults.

Angela, 15

At the moment 'greens' could easily be mistaken for boiled seaweed.

Sheila, 15

Whoever compiles the menus cannot have much of an idea of catering. A particular example of this is: green salad, fish, chips and peas. Ugh! I know that if it was left to me, or others that will remain anonymous, such a combination would not dare to cross the mind.

All this would be stopped in my ideal school, and pupils would have a menu of several dishes to choose from. I realize the possibility of unnecessary waste, but we could combat that by ordering the meal several days beforehand.

Valerie, 14

In my school nobody will force the pupils to eat if they don't want to. At the back of each age-room will be machines holding enough packed meals to feed everyone in the room. You put a sixpenny piece and a shilling in the machine and in return get an appetising packed lunch.

Girl, 14

If the food was meant to be hot it would be hot, and the jelly and fruit would be served on cold plates. (At my school the jelly is always melted by the time we can eat it because it is served on *hot* plates.)

Sylvia, 13

At dinner times no one would walk away from the canteen saying, 'What a rotten dinner, cannonball peas, fatty meat, uncooked potatoes, cold gravy, sickly pudding and water'; instead they would say, 'What a smashing dinner!' I am quite sure most mothers would not mind paying a little extra for their child's dinners if they knew that they were being improved. At the school I would like, there would be a choice and you could ask for a large or small dinner.

Susan, 14

A choice of dish only if it is from stringy beans to cannonball peas. The actual room could be bright and airy and the tables arranged in an orderly but not regular pattern.

Anne, 14

A menu I'd find delicious would consist of rice, meat, prawns and beans. For pudding, ice cream is very popular.

Clare, 11

Only nice dinners like mummy makes no sloppy peas or baked beans, no bacon and egg pie no cheese no onions and no heavy puddings. Custard would be thick and creamy we would have no chickin and piggy with broth not gravy and nice jellies with Dickinsons cream.

Gaye, 9 *

* An intruder to *The Observer* competition, but hardly to be omitted. Probably on no subject are small children so eloquent as on the subject of food.

Despotism Must Die

The trouble with considering discipline in schools as a separate topic is that it is not really detachable in this way. An unsatisfactory curriculum, dull teaching and unimaginative relationships between pupils and teachers make necessary the proliferation of petty rules; a bored and unhappy creature has to be kept in a cage. So what the children have to say about the way their schools are governed has to be related to their criticism in other areas.

Again, they want to be set free. It is not anarchy they want – as any honest teacher knows. Schoolchildren hate being out of control, obviously enough, because that turns schooling into a farce, and though any human being might welcome an interlude of farce, long periods of it are wearisome and demoralizing. I remember, during my own early teaching days when I could provide farce and little else, the notably ill-behaved boy who came to me after a lesson with a quiet complaint. 'Your lessons,' he said, 'give me a headache.' But control – any form of it worth having – is not obtained by a sort of panic and persecution of tiny rules. It never was so : it is less so than ever now that the general tone of our society has moved so far from authoritarianism. These essays are full of instances of school rules that are found irritating and pettifogging. I have quoted a few : the enforced silence where silence is not necessary or even helpful; the rule, so common, against staying in the building during lunchtimes and breaks; those rules designed to produce hollow 'good manners' which, as one child observes, cannot achieve ends that can result only from 'love and understanding' between members of a community. A typical rule of the latter kind, often found in boys' schools, is the one against having your hands in your pockets. As someone never at ease unless his hands are stowed in this way, I had many embarrassing moments as a teacher : at assemblies, or in corridors, when a colleague would bark, 'Take your hands out of your pockets', and umpteen boys and at least one master would sulkily obey. But almost any single instance of the rules that children protest against may seem trivial; it is the weight of them all, added together, and the attitudes that lie behind the making of them, that are important, and that raise the protest far above the level of triviality.

Especially the attitudes. As the children point out, it is such a one-way business. There is no argument about rules. The teachers know what is best. But responsible people are not created by imposing rules of conduct upon them, without discussion. Any rule that is not freely accepted, after debate, is likely to breed sullenness, furtive evasion. The children carry their argument very deep when they make, as many of them do, two particular points. The first is that anyone brought up for years under a regime that relies on an undiscussed network of rules is likely to lack self-discipline when he goes out into the world. He will have had no experience in helping to create a discipline for himself. The second point is that children of secondary school age are, at their best, rebellious creatures. It is the quality of the young, for which we should be properly grateful, that they scrutinize the world around them with fresh eyes and are intensely critical of what they see. Human advance depends on this new, rash discontent. It needs not frustrating with arbitrary rules but schooling in the discussion of the bases of reasonable conduct. That critical energy needs to be enlisted not alienated.

So the children reject the old authoritarian structure of the schools: corporal punishment certainly, rules on which they are never consulted, the prefect system which makes little tyrants out of other children and confines the exercise of responsibility to a minority. Aware of their own vigour, of the moral excitement and curiosity that are so marvellously strong in the young and are rejected and wasted when the staff alone lay down the law, they call for consultation. They want to be part of the government. 'Despotism in education must die !' It sounds almost melodramatic. But read what these children have to say, and then consider whether such a cry has any trace of exaggeration about it.

Too much emphasis is put on discipline nowadays. We are expected to keep many irritating and pointless rules out of loyalty for the school and awe of the school teachers. If schoolgoers were treated as responsible people, many rules could be abolished. School uniform is archaic, ugly, expensive and symbolic of the over-bearing attitude of teachers. If abolished, one cause of friction between pupils and staff would be destroyed.

Janet, 16

... **the importance of 'good manners'** is still being over-emphasized. Children are taught to respect the teacher, the older generation, by opening doors for them, standing when entering the room, for example. However, this tends to destroy a good child–teacher relationship. Love and understanding don't mean good manners; the love and understanding required in school is the love in a good relationship between child and teacher.

Valerie, 17

The days of 'hit and learn' are over. If a child is naturally dull, this cannot be helped. It will do him no good to be bullied.

Anthony, 15

I think it would be a very good idea to have less corporal punishment – as some of the methods these days are appalling, for instance when a teacher hits you with the strap it makes you mutter at them and it also makes you despise them all the more. I don't see no reason for it.

Frances, 12

All our teachers are allowed to belt and do so frequently. This makes the boys have competitions to see who can get belted more often.

Jane, 14

There would be no corporal punishment whatsoever, and if a pupil proved too much for the headmaster to handle because he or she was in some way disturbed, then a psychiatrist or social worker would be consulted, but no teacher would have the right to hit a pupil under any circumstances.

Ruth, 15

> Rules like rhyme schemes –
> designed to offer shape and movement to,
> and not restrict, subdue,
> the course of meaning.

W. (boy), 17

Another petty rule I would like to see done away with is the matter of hands in pockets. The rules call it sloppiness, but the Westerners do it and no one calls *them* sloppy.... I think that pupils should be allowed to play cards, etc., during breaks if they so wish. Recently the Head at my school condemned card games in school because school is primarily a place of work. It seems as though breaks are expected to be used as time for extra work, although there is nothing against other games played at these times.

If gambling is directly involved, then it should not be allowed as gambling is a form of corruption.

Louis, 15

To become interested in a subject the pupil has to enjoy it, and half the enjoyment of lessons is taken away if they are held in an enforced silence.

Gillian, 14

We would not be thrown out at lunchtime but would be allowed to go somewhere to sit and talk.

Janet, 14

Commonrooms with comfortable chairs, televisions, record players and other items should be where people would go ... after prep. Children should not be kicked out of every room they enter because one prefect or teacher happens to have a headache.

Eveline, 14

... **as at colleges and universities**, there would be a Students' Union. The students' commonroom would be comfortable, but there would also be a room where the pupils could listen to records, dance and make as much noise as they pleased.

Ian, 17

... **all too often the headmaster is an ogre-like figure** whose word is indisputable law. Pupils should be able to approach him in a corridor and speak openly to him, instead of having to go to a small office on the quiet side of the school.

Richard, 15

Bearing in mind that optimism leads to disappointment, I should be content to see a few small reforms in the running of schools. The one I should like most would be to place the supreme authority of the schools into the hands of a committee of, say, three head teachers, instead of leaving sole command to one headmaster or mistress, who often has to make major decisions quite impossible for one person to decide upon. Whatever the character of the head teacher, having final authority in a school of five hundred children must inevitably lead to a slight sense of superiority which would be greatly lessened by a policy of divided authority.

Sharon, 15

In this school the 'Big Powerful Headmaster' has no place, for no longer is he able to appoint, or dismiss, head boys, head girls and prefects, off his own bat; he has to consult the students' representatives. Neither he nor any member of his staff is able to deal out his or her own version of justice without the victim having the right to appeal against the sentence to a body consisting of both students and members of staff.

This sort of doctrine may seem absolutely misguided to fervent upholders of tradition, but I ask them – think! Is it any more than each adult has come to regard as his undeniable right? The principle that there must be freedom from a tyranny of the headmaster is applicable to all schools. Despotism in education must die.

Stephen, 17

I would like to see a student committee, with representatives for junior and senior parts of the school, in order to lobby the headmaster if anything (including teaching methods) was unsatisfactory. (If juniors found complaints, they should first be considered by chosen members of the sixth form.)

Alan, 16

Present-day schools are run by groups of people who don't really know the essentials of school problems. The people most directly concerned with the problems are never consulted. In the ideal school a group of the older boys and girls should be chosen by the other children as representatives, and this group of children should take over the duties of the governors. The children should, therefore, under the guidance of the head teacher, be virtually running the school themselves.

Brian, 16

... all this suggests that the school would be perpetually chaotic, which would give all the pupils an insight into what life, after school, is like: chaos.

Margaret, 14

If a problem could be rectified by pure discussion, then it most certainly would be, the object being that misbehaviour be dissuaded, not suppressed. Authority would be reasonable enough

158

not to prompt defiance, and if rebellion did break out, its futility would be demonstrated, not by castigation, but by rational argument.

There would be no prefects, or superior ranks of boys. Schoolboy persecution is a strong source of misery, and the frustration felt by boys at having to submit to the jurisdiction of others, superior to them only in age, provokes resistance.

Nicholas, 14

Prefects have rarely been chosen wisely, and seem to allow new powers to go to their heads. My ideal would be for the pupils to elect their own prefects. If a prefect was found to have overstepped his privileges several times, he could be made to appear in some sort of court proceedings before a jury of several boys and girls from each form. Also, when in this court, people will learn to argue to explain their ideas, so widening their horizons to learning concise speech and to trounce nonsense.

Richard, 15

Another thing that would not appear in a school I would like is a monitor system. These systems are wrong because, particularly in boys' school where senior boys have the power to beat younger boys, having power over others can give pupils an overbearing or even sadistic disposition. Besides, if one or a select body of persons is given all responsibilities, others do not have this chance. It is better to let the top forms help the staff in organizing functions and doing various chores to relieve the teachers. In this way, one and all would have a chance to develop commonsense, resourcefulness and reliability, to everyone's advantage.

Alexandra, 13

The Christian ideas taught in school include the evil of jealousy. Yet it is the prefect system that can easily cause unnecessary jealousy and ill-feeling between students. The younger pupils should not be brought up in an atmosphere where they are afraid of the older prefects; where they are afraid of other children. If this system were removed from schools by the powers-that-be, a great step forward would be achieved.

Valerie, 17

The discipline and life of the school would be based on freedom for the pupil. No uniforms and a minimum of control would be vital, and the pupils, male and female, would be treated as adults and allowed to see if they can live together in a community like intelligent people. Given this responsibility and freedom, the pupils would not obviously be always well-behaved and sensible, but they would, I believe, grow up to be mature and intelligent adults who are socially, and in all other respects, a benefit to the community.

Christopher, 16

Teenagers, nearly all of whom are haters of discipline, dream of a school where no rules are made, no uniform is worn and where they can do as they please. They must realize that discipline has to be enforced to keep any school in order. Although I have dreams of such places, I try to ignore them and imagine a school, with luxuries, which can still serve its correct purpose.

Sheila, 15

I would like punishment to become a kind of reflex action. There would obviously be certain places in the school where silence was necessary, and a half hour detention would be the normal punishment for breaking this rule. The detention would be given as automatically as a cashier gives a receipt – with neither doubt nor malice. Working in the school gardens might prove a suitable punishment for other crimes.

Rachel, 17

Petty rules are irksome and make for irritability, and if a pupil is always told what to do he will be lost when faced with an outside decision or dilemma. It is much more pleasant to have a trusting and free atmosphere than one where the pupils are expected to do wrong and must be corrected.

Alexandra, 13

Complaints about the school from pupils should be turned into criticism about the school by tactful form teachers.

Kari, 13

There would be no gaps between the pupils and the staff as there is in practically all schools. The pupils would organize the running of the school along with the staff so the school was more the sort of place the pupils wanted it to be. Due to this scheme the pupils would take a more lively interest in the activities of the school as they would choose and organize them (with some help from the staff) themselves.

Ruth, 15

Yes, school is not just a world full of teachers teaching dopey children, children must co-operate as well, and the school should be a happy place.

Rosemary, 13

My school of the future would be one in which the individual would be free and there would be people as distinct from hordes of children. (How derogatory that term 'child' has become!) Does anyone advocate freedom in the schools as vociferously as is done for, say, the pirate radio ships? Freedom to think and learn is as important to us as food, yet I am afraid that it is as scarce in our schools as food is in some parts of the world!

Dermot, 17

I would like to see self-government by the pupils. I suggest a sort of committee made up of pupils of each age group and elected by that age group. To this committee could go grievances and complaints. At a weekly (or fortnightly) meeting of the whole school these would be dealt with and punishment meted out by the committee. Although the punishments could not be severe, the shame of being publicly accused would act as a deterrent for the future. In serious cases, e.g. stealing, which the committee felt they were incapable of dealing with, then (and only then) would the matter be referred to the staff. In the present system the culprit is caught and punished by the teachers. I do not believe that this almost secretive form of punishment is effective enough.

Of course, this system of mine would only work if all the pupils co-operated. One of the main drawbacks would be the possibility of victimization of the punished pupils by the others. However, I think that well over ninety per cent would be too sensitive to do anything of this nature. The system would give the pupils a greater sense of honesty and responsibility when they go out in the world. At the moment the majority of school leavers have been disciplined for the past thirteen or fourteen years. In my opinion they are not able to take up a life outside, where they must think for themselves and rely on their own judgement and integrity.

Susan, 16

Youths from twelve to eighteen years of age are the most rawly aware, most dissatisfied and most rebellious age group in society. As soon as such and such an activity is compulsory, it becomes an unattractive thing to do. If every school activity is optional, even the boy who always 'hated' sport will go to a games lesson 'just to see what it's like', and probably attend again when he finds that it's fun even when one does badly, as long as one takes everything in good heart.

The staff would have to be ready to accept almost anything, from watching a boy read a German novel throughout French lessons for a week, to giving incessant homework to a girl who has nothing to do at home. Even the most rebellious pupils would be found to be quite quiet and well-behaved, simply because they feel that they could escape at any moment should they wish it.

There is no feeling of being fenced in, which can send the delicate and developing emotions of a teenager into frantic tempers and tension.

Vanessa, 17

Because the young 'have never had it so good', they are enjoying freedom other generations did not. The tragedy is that all the energy and drive that accompanies this freedom is largely misapplied, *against* society. Something is required to bridge the gap between school and society – a college where reaction is almost encouraged in order to exorcise it before the individual has to hold responsibility in society. With increasingly fewer class barriers, youth is steadily becoming a unified anti-social movement, when in fact to be 'at odds' with society is probably only an expression of fear of that society. A new form of education is needed to prevent youth from trying to segregate itself further from society.

Simon, 18

I Know How Other Children Feel

The music department would be in the shape of a violoncello, the music books being kept in the thinner part of the building, and the remainder of the rooms having instruments which pupils could learn.

Sally, 14

The examinations would be done by a machine and a man. The pupil would be fastened into a chair and have wires affixed to his head. The back of the chair would then be lowered so that the pupil would be in a lying position. The man would then check that the pupil was comfortable and, if so, his head would be placed in a glass dome. The machine would then be turned on and after a quarter of an hour a percentage would appear on a screen. The percentage would be the amount of knowledge that the pupil had taken in over that time. If the total was not high enough the pupil would be 'brainwashed', so that he knew enough. Brainwashing would be suitable as a method for teaching as the brain would not be active enough.

Jean, 12

In my perfect school there would *not* be a lot of visiting people coming to try out experiments on us and, in general, treating us like a lot of human guineapigs! That sounds a bit biassed, but that's what I think.

Isabel, 11

In geography instead of sitting down and reading about Africa, the form master or robot would press a few certain buttons and away the class would go off to Africa. They would stay there overnight and study Africa at close quarters.

Harry, 13

The needlework, housecraft and any other craft lessons, I think, should be equipped with a wireless, because I myself can concentrate more while a wireless is on.

Rachel, 15

I think the education committee might allow my school to be built if they like it and also if it didn't cost too much. As a rough estimate I would say it would cost at least £5000. But the committee might say, 'Britain can't afford that much money to waste on a building. Even if it is a school.' If they said this I would write a letter telling them that Mr Wilson spends more than that in a week. This might make them change their minds and agree to build my ideal school.

Leone, 13

For practical lessons, such as art or needlework, the pupil can turn on one of the computer's eyes. This eye keeps a close watch on the pupil's progress and the computer groans loudly if the pupil makes a mistake.

The computer also reads literature books out loud and the pupil listens carefully. (The computer has an adjustable voice, so when the pupil gets tired of one voice, he can alter it.)

Lindsay-Jane, 15

I would like my school to be called Saint Monica's and if possible to be situated in the Austrian Alps.

Colette, 13

Young students especially become disheartened when taught by erudite professors.

Boy, 15

At the school I'd like, pupils over the age of eleven would earn a salary. A child aged eleven of average intelligence could earn

15s a month – his or her salary to be raised each year according to his or her intelligence until a boy or girl of eighteen with a high standard of intelligence could earn £5 a month.

Sylvia, 13

I have chosen a grammar school as the school I like as they usually have a higher proportion of intelligent children or at least children who do well at academic subjects. There are times when I talk to children from other types of school when I feel half ashamed of being intelligent and enjoying school.

It may be reactionary of me, but I am all in favour of streaming. All the children in one form being of a similar level of intelligence seems to me to make it far easier to progress rapidly. Apart from that, it's very irritating to have to explain myself to the not-so-intelligent, in fact downright dumb kids. My mother's friends seem to specialize in producing this type in large quantities, so I have enough of them at weekends and in the evenings without having to undergo similar miseries in school.

Katherine, 12

The initial reason [for having a college intermediate between school and university] is to kill off the miserable race of sixth formers who sit writing out the same copious notes and, like so many blotting paper creations, soak up information only for duplication on examination paper.

Simon, 18

We will take our trip,
   drink milk with wise, friendly men,
   and go home to read.

Richard, 17

Sixth formers have too many opportunities to themselves. For instance, nearly every play is sixth formers.

David, 15

Prizes should be done away with as it is only the chosen few (the same pupils year after year who receive the prizes and sit smugly at the top of the form) who have more share of brains than the remainder of the idiots sitting in the front row.

Carol, 16

Speech Day I would like to see abolished because it is no benefit to anyone – it is embarrassing for prizewinners and boring for the other pupils.

Carrol, 15

Work standards should be rewarded relative to the individual's average ability, not to the competitive standard of the class as a whole. That is, if my usual grade is E and I produce a much better piece of work I would be awarded an A; whereas if Mr Brains (of average ability A) produced a sub-standard piece for him – even though it is better than mine – he would only get a C.

Ian, 16

The ideal place to be dreamed,
By architects, planners and surveyors;
A building so ugly and large – but they say
It would answer all our prayers.
Comprehension, they tell us, is the ideal state;
With co-operation between teachers and pupils alike.
Plenty of work, plenty of play,
And no one on strike.
A fair chance our children must get.
Yet these blind fools will never know
What goes on inside this dreaded place –
Some cheat, some work, some sleep, some fret,
Some soar high, others low,
Just to emerge at last
As one of the human race.

R. (boy), 15

Essentially school must be a part of family life, and for this reason day schools the usual form of school. For how will a teenager, if unable at this stage of his life to combine school and home life, be able to cope with the frustrations and difficulties of life later?

Mary, 14

We wouldn't make silly stuffed animals for babies we would make mod clothes for our dollies.

We would be taught how to drive a car and sensible things like that, how to cook nice things not fish.

We wouldn't have any bullies like Charles Ward and Carol Brown or any show offs like Robina and Elaine. Who always say my daddy's done this my daddy's done that he's been on T.V. and he smokes a pipe and we have bought this and that and are going here and there seen this and that etc silly things.

Our school would have every room painted differently our classroom would be purple and white.

We would go on holiday abroad and also to the tower of London and have tea with the Queen and Prince Andrew and if Prince Philip was good and not playing at Polo he could come and have a cherry bun with pink icing.

Gaye, 9 *

I would like a school that did not tell you off much and when it did tell you off theyd only tell you what youd done wrong and not to do it again. They only say your nauty you shouldnt have done it but quite often we dont know what weve done wrong.

i wold like a school that some times let you writ out work for other children in other schools. i wold like it espesherly becos i get tiyed of having work givern to me to do and i think as i am a child that i now how other children feel and so i can make it eseyer for them and its youshuly only seniers that visit other schools and hospitals and places but we now just as much as seniers and if we cold visit all these places wed now how other

---

* Gaye, who entered for the competition because her bossy sister did, and Kirsty (on page 170), whose mother said she was 'most enthusiastic to set her views down', are irresistible intruders.

children feel a lot more and i think it wold be nice if we cold sugest things for ourselvs to do.

wy cant we have one lesson for each day and coldent we keep our own clay and stuff, and coldent we have classes of speshel things like modling, music, poims, and dansing of diforent cinds wich we cold ches to do. id like us to have more natur lessons out side and id prefer not to keep together as animals dont come out wen thers lots of peopel.

Kirsty, 7 *

Once more back to the similar stark classrooms,
School times are the best times of your life?
Youth, school, do they mix?
It's beautiful to get older.
School is always there
To be hated, loved,
To comfort, to hurt,
To help, to hinder.

Alizoun, 13

... there is an acute danger of a few select and progressive institutions being labelled as typical of the modern British educational system, whilst slum schools still remain and others exist inadequately staffed and equipped.

Mary, 16

Parents like to think they have a say in how their children are educated. Before the eleven plus they all fill in a form stating what schools they would prefer their children to go to in the event of their failing or passing the 'great exam'.

This is in fact the only way in which parents can exercise their volition. Once their children are at their secondary school, the teachers have absolute power. When parents state the schools of their preference, they choose those with a good reputation and examination record. Rarely do they have any idea of how the schools are run, and what their offspring might think of the teaching methods. Parents do reserve the right to complain, of course, but are reluctant to do so for fear of making matters worse for their children. I would make parent associations lively and really influential. An arbitrary body should be set up to deal with complaints. School students, like university students, should play a greater part in the running of the school.

Janet, 16

Eyes, like worms that crawl with no mercy over one of those,
Those who find pleasure in an air of shabby clothes and hair.
Eyes that condemn as ignorance these ideas, and in front of the
    world interrogate, and cast to dogs.
How can one receive education from those who do but push
    forward criticism?
We must wait, with probing hope, for some particle of this tiring
    older race to convert.
Convert from those who can but fight between theirselves, to the
    race who will conquer bad and bring forth peace.
So why should we try to take education from those who us despise.
Let us rebel, us the opposed, and cast out these wage pulling civil
    criticizers and form our own schools.
The which teach the beauty of all rough and tidy.
Please excuse spelling, no one will educate me.

Nigel, 14

Other Penguin Education Specials

Children in Distress

Alec Clegg and Barbara Megson

Two out of every hundred children have to be given direct help by the State – whether it be psychiatric, social or medical.

But are these the only children 'in distress'? What about those children who do not qualify for State help?

Alec Clegg and Barbara Megson estimate that perhaps 12 per cent of our children desperately need help, but do not qualify to receive it. *Children in Distress* paints an agonizing picture of child distress, based on the authors' long experience in educational administration. They argue that it is the schools – in daily contact with the children – that are the agencies best suited to help this large and saddening section of our child population.

'... this book, containing a wealth of information and ideas based on the experience of very many schools, can help teachers who want to help their problem pupils, but just do not know how to start. It can help them, probably, more than any other single volume.'
The Times Educational Supplement

Education for Democracy

Edited by David Rubenstein and Colin Stoneman

The time for a radical manifesto on British education is long
overdue. For over twenty-five years the struggle to democratize
our system has been held back by those who see the proper
function of education as the production of an elite and, as the most
efficient means of effecting this, the labelling of children as As or
Ds at the earliest possible opportunity. Those children who do not
meet the requirements of the current elite have had some reason to
be disconsolate about their fate.

Here at last – appropriately at a time when the 'backlash' is
receiving all the attention, if not actually gaining the upper hand –
is a bold definition of the nature and purpose of 'education for
democracy'.

The contributors to this collection, all of whom have to grapple
daily with these problems on the lecture-hall or classroom floor, do
not attempt to put forward a single, easy solution. But whether
they are writing about the content of the primary curriculum or
university examinations, about slum schools or the new technology
of learning, there is one fundamental belief which they all hold in
common. They demand an education system which cares about *all*
children, regardless of race, class or intelligence, and which helps to
build a democratic society by upholding the qualities of compassion
and respect within its own walls.

'The most radical reply to the Black Paper ...' *Education*

'...a thought-provoking and stimulating book...' *Tribune*

Letter to a Teacher

The School of Barbiana

Eight young Italian boys from the mountains outside Florence wrote this passionate and eloquent book. It took them a year. Simply and clearly, with some devastating statistical analysis of the Italian education system, they set out to show the ways in which attitudes towards class, behaviour, language and subject-matter militate against the poor. They describe, too, the reforms they propose, and the methods they use in their own school – the School of Barbiana, started under the guidance of a parish priest and now run entirely by the children.

This remarkable book was written for the parents of the Italian poor. But it is about the poor everywhere: their anger is the anger of every worker and peasant who sees middle-class children absorbed effortlessly into the schools as teacher's favourites.

Letter to a Teacher was a best-seller in Italy and has been published subsequently in many languages. The School of Barbiana was awarded the prize of the Italian Physical Society, usually reserved for promising physicists, for the statistical achievement involved in the book.

'Hearing this passionate, angry cry from a few poor boys in a remote Italian region, we dare not and must not dismiss it as an interesting and exotic but irrelevant social happening in a country whose problems are not ours. These boys *are* ours; their counterparts are talking or shouting in school after school, on campus after campus, the same message into our ears. We must learn soon, while we still have time, to hear what they say.' *John Holt*

'The Pre-School Years deserves serious and urgent attention,
and the author is to be congratulated on a wise, lively and valuable
piece.... It deals one of the most telling blows in the long and
doughty battle waged for the four million under-fives who still
remain outside the recognized educational system.'
The Times Educational Supplement

The Pre-School Years is about the education of children during the
most crucial period in their intellectual and emotional development,
their first five years, and the virtually irreversible nature of the
changes which are nurtured in the pre-school child. Most
importantly, it is about the extraordinary educational neglect of
these children in a society which acknowledges their importance.

This new edition of this widely acclaimed book has been completely
revised, and startling evidence has been added on the biological
value of play in the early years, on the physical provision of
pre-school education, and on a number of experiments in the
running of nursery schools by local communities.